3

TEMPORARY HOMELANDS

TEMPORARY
HOMELANDS

A L I S O N
H A W T H O R N E
D E M I N G

MERCURY HOUSE ◆ SAN FRANCISCO

Published in the United States by
Mercury House
San Francisco, California

Grateful acknowledgement goes to the following publications in which some of these essays first appeared: "An Island Notebook," The Georgia Review, Winter 1991; "Sidecuts," Sonora Review, Spring 1993; and "Claiming the Yard," Sierra, 1994. "An Island Notebook" also appeared in *The Pushcart Prize, XVIII: Best of the Small Presses,* 1993.

UNITED STATES CONSTITUTION, FIRST AMENDMENT: Congress shall make no law respecting an establishment of religion, or prohibiting the free exercise thereof; or abridging the freedom of speech, or of the press; or the right of the people peaceably to assemble, and to petition the Government for a redress of grievances.

Mercury House and colophon are registered trademarks of
Mercury House, Incorporated

Printed on recycled, acid-free paper
Manufactured in the United States of America

LIBRARY OF CONGRESS CATALOGING-IN-PUBLICATION DATA
Deming, Alison Hawthorne, 1946–
        Temporary Homelands / Alison Hawthorne Deming.
        p.   cm.
        ISBN 1-56279-062-5
        1. Human ecology. 2. Human ecology — Religious aspects.
I. Title
GF49.D46 1994
304.2—dc20   93-41676
                                                  CIP

5   4   3   2   1
FIRST EDITION

*This book is for
Lucinda Bliss,
my daughter,
friend,
and fellow artist*

CONTENTS

Acknowledgments   ix
Preface   xi

I
An Island Notebook   5
The Perfect Hike   24
Sidecuts   38

II
Inside the Wolf   51
Exiled in America   74
Woods Work   95

III
The Chaco Phenomenon   113
The Petrified Forest   129
Claiming the Yard   142

IV
Wolf, Eagle, Bear: An Alaska Notebook   149
The Nature of Poetry: Poetry in Nature   176
Eagle Transforming into Itself   191

ACKNOWLEDGMENTS

I GIVE HEARTFELT THANKS TO THE PEOPLE AND PLACES who nourished this work. At times, the writing felt like a collective enterprise—the words, spirit, faith, and friendship of others weaving in and out of my mind to feed me. In particular, for the inspiration of their own work and their encouragement of mine, I thank W. S. Di Piero, Gary Paul Nabhan, Richard Nelson, Philip Booth, John Daniel, Joanne Mulcahy, Carolyn Servid, Robert Michael Pyle, Roger Swain, Richard Shelton, Benjamin Alire Sáenz, and Karla Elling. I thank Karen Falkenstrom for putting out the fires I set at work while my attention was drawn into this book. I thank Stephen Corey at *The Georgia Review* for accepting and carefully editing the first of these essays. I thank Lucinda Bliss and Boyer Rickel for their attentive and insightful readings of earlier versions of this work. Jennifer McDonald and Tom Christensen made the book possible by believing in it well before they had good reason to—*thank you.*

I haven't lived anywhere long enough to be anything other than an outsider. To those who shared their places and stories with me, especially to the people of Grand Manan, the place that comes closest to a homeland for me, thank you. To those who spoke casually to me one day and may be surprised to find a version of their words in these pages, please forgive my acquisitive nature. My intentions have been generous—not to appropriate other people's stories, but to understand how our separate stories color each other, and how they are shaped by the gifts of friendship and conversation.

For gifts of time and other support, which enabled me to complete this book, I am grateful to the Corporation of Yaddo; the Island Institute in Sitka, Alaska; the University of Arizona; and the Tucson/Pima Arts Council.

PREFACE

NATURE, THE TANGLED COMMUNITY OF LIFE ON EARTH
—in all its complexity, beauty, ugliness, violence, and plasticity—
has never felt anything less than miraculous to me. An energy
seems to glow in the things of nature that wakes an inner dimension in me. Because I cannot explain this phenomenon and I cannot manipulate or control it, I call it spiritual. Even the concept of
evolution heightens, for me, this sense of the spiritual in nature by
marrying the fragile thingness of the body to something immortal
inside it. I began writing these essays as a way to explore the tension I have felt between my own love and fear of nature, between
my admiration for our species and my concern for our future,
between the harmony I seek in going into the wilds and the general
disharmony with the natural world that our culture has created.

I wanted to write an honest book about my relationship with
nature—not to offer theories or prescriptions for what that relationship ought to be. I wanted to examine how I actually experience nature, not by defining it, but by engaging with it as an
ongoing process of encounter and by making it show itself as a process rooted in family and cultural history. I wanted to understand
the places, events, and ideas in my own experience that seem most
significant in shaping that relationship, and to explore the quality
of reflection that certain loved places seem to induce. This book,
finally, is about one thing—reconstructing an intimacy with
nature. We live in a time of radical loss—loss of space, places,
tribes, and species. Loss of a sense of belonging in and to a place.

Loss of continuity and coherence. We live with a painful sense that the human species is the most destructive force on the planet. Even so, the fact ironically remains that we are embedded in nature. Every second of every day we are in relationship with that force— it is what we are.

In front of my home in Tucson, Arizona, stands a fat palm tree big enough to have been planted in 1938 when this house was built. The young palm fronds fan out from a high crown, the old ones dying, drying, and drooping against the trunk like a skirt. The dense flounce of brown stalks holding onto the tree makes a fine bird habitat, and the tree is constantly busy with pigeons, Inca doves, and cactus wrens. Every couple of years a fierce wind rips the dead fronds apart and a heap of a dozen or so falls to the ground in an apocalypse of thorny deadwood, shit-splattered leaves, and nesty wads of grass—the ruined city. Bald nestlings squawk then stiffen on the hot, dry ground. The neighborhood cats have a field day. The mature birds set right to work. They seem to have a special song for this apocalyptic time. It is characteristically beautiful. I cannot hear the grief in their singing. Or their exhaustion. I don't know whether my species is capable of hearing such things in the language of another. I watch them rebuild and I know it's my job to learn to listen much more carefully.

TEMPORARY HOMELANDS

ONE

 # AN ISLAND NOTEBOOK

JULY 15

Today the water is glass, barely a ripple to disrupt the view so wide I swear the horizon describes the earth's great curve. The Bay changes daily, its surface reworked by the wind and currents. It can be a dappled tweed, or riled up and spiked with whitecaps, or this liquid mercury so smooth and viscous a seiner cuts a gentle mile-long wake, one line of the V bending nearly into an S as it meets an opposing current. One could make a vocation of studying the patterns and find it less routine than most jobs. On the margin, Swallowtail Lighthouse turns its eye out into the dusk, scans back over the brush weir staked offshore below the spruce-topped cliffs. The structure is graceful, and the weir works to catch the abundant herring that have made many islanders rich. On one of the adjacent even smaller islands there are three millionaires. I learned this from a bird-watcher I met there who had set down his tripod in the wild caraway to look for the puffins or razorbill auks that frequent the outlying rocks. He had once studied botany and knew the scientific names of several local species. An investment broker in Saint John, who owns a share in The Mumps—a large double weir staked near the harbor—so I had reason to trust his authority on the matter.

In front of our cottage there's a road, for many years the only tarred one on fifteen miles of rock, spruce, and balsam. There are five villages strung along the eastern side of the island. Cars race back and forth between them. Someone delivers an old rocking chair to his brother, brings her husband to work on the fishermen's wharf, calls at the nursing home, or runs up to North Head to meet the ferry. I've wished for years the road wasn't there, since I come here to get calm and clear. But it's the noisy compromise required to return year after year to just this view. And there are quiet places—almost everywhere else but the house is quiet enough that I can hear the breeze chafe the August-dry stalks of grass, water lick the rocks, or mackerel boil in shallow water as they are pursued toward shore by feeding dolphins. What I know of the place after thirty-five years of returning is that it engenders a state of mind like no other. The experience is a species in danger of being lost.

The first year I was eight, and my family had read a magazine article about budget vacations. The Finger Lakes. Cayman Islands. Grand Manan. Before that we'd gone for our two weeks to Nantucket and rented a house named Little Nest. My father fished for crabs in a tidal stream, and my mother indulged me by driving to the bayside, where I could wade and collect the golden pandora shells. My brother caught poison ivy, preferred the surf, and fought with someone every day until he cried out for help, lodged up in a tree, a stick embedded in his eyeball. When that island got too crowded and too expensive (the two so often occur simultaneously), we went farther north. Going north simplifies things—fewer people, fewer industries, fewer comforts. I remember driving through an eternity of spruce, miles of it burned black and skeletal. I remember the car getting searched at the border and losing an hour. I remember having lunch across the street from a branch of the Hudson's Bay Company while we waited for the ferry to load our Studebaker with a sling and a winch. I remember knowing I was very far from home.

July 24
This morning Lester, my neighbor, shows up. It's his week off from Coastal Transport—the ferry terminal at North Head—so he has

time for the side jobs that keep him equipped with a new pickup and ATV. Workers on the island answer to the schedule of season and tide. In June, men stitch twine onto the weir stakes; July and August, they go out seining—do it at 3 A.M. if that's when the tide is right. By September, women clean the smoked herring at boning tables, pack ten pounds of the leathery strips in each wooden crate. At neap tide the unemployed pick periwinkles and dulse, an edible purple seaweed that is dried crisp in the sun. A few punch the clock of government jobs—fisheries, post office, liquor store. And the ferry. But island time—work time—is a neighborly joke. If Lester says he'll be here next week to do the job, that means sometime in the next three months. Then, there he'll be—7 A.M.—leaning his ladder against the bedroom window of this poor, sleeping vacationer and singing like a meadowlark.

Today, replacing the cedar shingles on the south side of our cottage, he sets loose a handful of bats that have been nesting in the eaves. Fur plush as a seal's, little pink triangle of mouth rimmed with saw-blade teeth, legs doing double duty as stays in their wings. Brown skin silky, translucent. They shriek from the light, then fall dormant as if it's a toxin, scrambling lamely to hide under the heap of rotted shingles or slither under the sill into the cellar. As more tumble down from the staging, I scoop them onto a shingle and flick it to set them flying. They don't go far, falling drugged into the raspberry patch. "I'd kill them for you," says Lester, "except they eat their weight in blackflies in a day." They keep screeching from their hiding places as I get near—parents and their young ones, we figure, and they don't like the looks of me. Lester hammers and sings, "Once more with feeling, then let's call it an afternoon."

The bats have lived here for generations—far longer than I've been coming. In the evening they'd wake up, zipping faster as the dark deepened, their flight patterns erratic and voracious. They drove my cat crazy. And they charmed an older couple who once rented the cottage. Instead of cocktails, they had the bats at the end of the day, setting the porch chairs out on the lawn where they could watch them comb the air, the woman often walking among them, letting them swirl around her head. I'm going to hate telling them that I've evicted the tenants, but the shingling project left no choice: leave the wood to rot, the process enhanced by composting bat shit, or rout them out and repair. Their young have been raised here year after year. It's been a peaceful place, people in the house for only a few months. Every choice is a loss. I will miss them.

JULY 26

9:15 A.M. The phone rings. It's Ann. "We finally got our good day!" We agree on the eleven-thirty boat to White Head Island, a free mail boat that runs the half-hour passage; once a skow lashed to a seiner, it's now a proper ferry capable of carrying a dozen cars. The skow's gone and so is most of the white head—granite blasted out last summer to build a breakwater and extend the fishermen's harbor. In years to come tourists will ask why they call it White Head, and people will have forgotten the reason. They'll call it Breakwater Island or Broken Head. At least here the progress is slow.

The White Head smokehouses are working. Racks of glistening herring hang, dripping golden oil, the meat browning in the controlled heat of a sawdust fire. A few miles offshore, a huge Russian factory ship, rumored to employ three hundred men, lies at anchor, processing the catch through day and night, diesel exhaust clouding its air. There's no lack of market this year. We bike past the harbor to where the asphalt peters out into a gravel road, and from there to the great smile of an empty sand beach on the island's backside.

Ann and Mike are summer people. Recidivists like myself. Retirement and the physical concessions of aging haven't deterred them from loving the remote places. Every winter they camp in the Anza-Borrego Desert, and summers they come here, Ann swimming daily into the ocean off one stony beach or another, though the water is chilled by the Labrador Current year-round. It's her daily communion. Berrying is Mike's. He keels on arthritic legs, grazing into the patches with two containers slung on strings around his neck (one for wild raspberries, the other for gooseberries), wading into the sweetness that takes over the border zones between spruce woods and human habitation. He could die in the berries, I think, and it would be a short fall from there into timelessness. It's not greed that keeps him knee-deep in the tangled canes for days on end. Half the time he picks to give them away, going down to the fishermen's pier at evening and coming back with a whole flounder or pollock, next day repaying the debt with a quart of red raspberries. Any bramble of the beauties is fair game, though sometimes a landowner will barrel out to warn Mike he's on private land. Then he'll say, "Well, gee, these berries are ready and no one's picking them. I'll give them to you—I just pick for the pleasure of picking." It's his meditation—centering on the moment of ripeness, here and here and here.

After a picnic lunch, Ann and I hike to the bog lake to swim, our feet sponging into the deep sphagnum of the trail. The water is a clear, rusty tea—contaminated only with tannin, a clean vegetable compound, an astringent that closes skin wounds and invigorates the pores. The bog is a primeval place inhabited by carnivorous sundews, their spatulate leaves rimmed with red glandular hairs that each hold a bead of clear sap for enticing and trapping prey. Minuscule orchids and pitcher plants.

Ann and I strip down, wade into the sandy mahogany muck until we can slip our whiteness into the perfect cool, and glide to the center of the pond, floating on our backs to admire the glistening cattail reeds that fringe the shore. Mike's gone off for the gooseberries that favor the gritty soil beside the gravel road.

JULY 29

I used to think I loved the island for its wildness—the transcendentalist's dream of a place so wild that by virtue of its wildness it's more civilized. But human culture here fascinates as much as nature, the way the place and its people are as much one thing as form and content in a painting by Paul Klee.

A woman moved here from Toronto after making documentaries, traveling to China and Russia and stopping people on the streets of New York to ask what they dream about, what they wish for. "A farm," so many of them had said, and they could picture the color of the bedroom curtains.

Gleason Green, who at ninety-two can recite Robert Service poems and anonymous ballads. "That reminds me of a story," he says, stroking his palm, his eyes rolling up, the slurring cadence of his island accent a sweet transport back in time. "Some men came down from Newfoundland to sell fish. We asked them what their lives were like. Hard, they said. They traded seals for flour, sugar, and clothes." Then he ricochets off into another story, "You know what a serenade is?" Telling how at a wedding party they used to blast off shotguns and dynamite caps outside the window. Once some guy blew his hand apart, but it was still a funny story. No elegy. Just the way it was. With a little encouragement, he tells how the Chrysler Corporation invited him to Detroit to tour the plant after he'd bought over three hundred motors for custom-built fishing boats. He used to make charter runs out to Kent and Machias Seal Islands, cooking up chowder and blueberry pie on board for the tourists. He earned a slot in *Reader's Digest*—"My Most Unforgettable Character." Twenty years later he still gets a few fan letters each month.

My father tells the story about a logging company coming to the island and offering the men wages of five dollars an hour, rain or shine, when they were lucky to make a dollar an hour for fishing. The company proposed to log off the island's balsam and spruce— a forest that sprawls over the majority of its interior. A meeting was called. The locals asked the company officials to give them half an hour alone to make their decision. Their answer: "If there's fish we'll catch them, and if there aren't, we won't." The forest remains intact except for a few building lots, areas thinned out from harvesting weir stakes, and an unsightly gouge cut for the new airstrip, which looks like a barber's mistake.

The airport is progress, of course, and the people wouldn't have allowed it unless they were certain it would benefit the island: provide a faster market for the salmon being raised in experimental aquaculture; lure back the Japanese market for sea urchins, beach dross that for a few years the islanders had turned into VCRs and Camaros; bring relatives home for the weekend and get the ailing off to medical care. Still, it's hard for anyone who's seen her hometown overtaken by malls, or his farm broken down into a trailer park or, worse, for its pretense of "value," into a gaggle of condominiums, not to look on the airstrip with a fearful eye. Even the innkeepers agree they don't really want any more tourists.

The sling-and-winch car ferry to Grand Manan is gone. No doubt it was a deterrent to the more frivolous travelers, being a refitted minesweeper from the Second World War. And to witness one's precious means of conveyance, loaded with the family's vacation cache, get hoisted by a derrick over the side of a pier was not everyone's idea of a relaxing getaway. The newer, ramped vessel— the *Grand Manan IV*—instead of embarking from the genteel tourist town of St. Andrews, leaves the New Brunswick mainland from Blacks Harbour. It's a working-class village, home of Connors Brothers, The World's Largest Sardine Industry—or so boasts the only billboard in town. Identical cheap small houses, Connors School, Connors IGA, and most likely Connors graveyard. There's no lunch counter here. Just a take-out trailer at the end of a dead-end road where travelers can buy strong tea and a greasy fish sandwich while waiting for the ferry to arrive. For those who live here, the landscape surrounding the town must offer consolation for the limits of daily life: the deep cove speaking of shelter at sea, the stands of balsam and spruce of shelter on shore. The view out to the expanding channel and the uninhabited islets called The Wolves speaks the language of daydreams. Clusters of goldenrod harbor sleeping bees, apparently tranquilized by gorging on pollen.

Part of our family story about Grand Manan is that when you get on board at Blacks Harbour and the ferry slips out into the channel, you leave your problems behind, see them drop away with the view of the mainland. This year, while the scenery fell into the distance, a woman twenty years younger than I climbed up the diamond-plate steel stairway from the car deck to the lounge, her unresponsive feet lifted one by one by her sister, who was coming up behind her. Two men followed carrying her folded wheelchair and, when they'd all reached the passenger deck, helped her get situated for the two-hour boat ride. I wondered, how did it happen, how long has she been that way, will she always remain so? How is it different to have the body become uncooperative when you're young as opposed to when you're old like my father, who is struggling at eighty-four to recover from a major stroke? This new-formed constellation of nature, limitation, and decline all circling in my mind—this learning to live not with hope or despair but with what is. The obligation to survive.

AUGUST 1
Hiking the Red Trail from Whale Cove to Ashburton Head. I follow the cliff line, watching the cloud bank thicken and rile up the Bay. The wind carries the perfume of balsams, released when the bud caps are forced off by the pale fists of new growth. Tattered drapes of gray moss hang from the foggy evergreens. Below, fish schools swarm in the clear water, moving as birds do, as if with one mind, the shape of their society forming, deforming, and reforming as fluidly as clouds or a symphony. I don't want to see a single person today. Want no human gabble to clutter my wavelengths, want only to experience myself in relation to a place, to

natural forces, to this molded spiral of paper the wasps have made—chewing up cellulose and spitting it out to build their hive. Handmade paper—the kind a few haiku could be penned on. I'm grateful for the invention of paper, which allows me to chew experience and spit out a structure I can live with. But get a human being in the act and too often the enterprise inflates. I remember reading that a paper manufacturer once developed a fine-grade stationery by appropriating the muslin in which ancient mummies had been wrapped.

Fireweed. Boneset. Pearly everlasting. Wildflowers thriving in a pool of light opened by a fallen spruce. The trail is rough, the ground spongy. A matted heath. There are ancient plants—horsetail (tiny versions of a Carboniferous period tree) and delicate Indian pipes (waxy white saprophytes also known as ghost flowers). And somewhere in these woods there is no doubt a plant just evolving, to which no one has affixed a name.

AUGUST 5

Saturday. 9 A.M. The Farmer's Market. A half-court lot with a rusted hoop, located between the old town hall and a closed movie theater—both now used mostly for rummage sales. Two pickups selling fresh garden produce, others selling handknit sweaters, quilts, framed color photos of the island, lemon meringue tarts, oat bran bread, and used books. I get my week's quota of greens, consider Ellman's biography of Yeats and a collection of Leonard Cohen's poetry. A well-dressed couple sit on a prefab park bench stroking guitars and singing hymns. At the other end of the parking lot, Harry Green, a gaunt dulse-picker and winner of some backwater songwriter-of-the-year award, stands beside a display of cassettes, his expression ghostly intent while the tape plays out his life story.

Bud Brown, a rugged oak of a fisherman I've known since we were kids, gives me a nod. He says everything's gone downhill since his kids brought home a black cat two years ago—no herring in Brown's Weir, and the Maine Pearl Company, which used to buy scales from him, has shut down, overstocked, for the year. He doesn't even take his pumper out when they go to tend the weir. The Russian factory ship hasn't helped him. The Mumps is making millionaires. But the Mystery Weir isn't worth a trip out. Why do they call it that, I ask, because it's a mystery what they'll pull out of there? Could be, he says, or else it's a mystery how so many families have lived on it all these years. Ownership of the weirs, like the old whalers, is by shares. And while the method is ancient—handed down from the Micmac and Passamaquoddy, who built brush traps along the shore—the expense is a risky contemporary proposition. A family may invest twenty thousand dollars or more in building a weir and make nothing for five years running. Then, if the herring run right and the market's good, in a day they can pay off the weir, the car, and the mortgage.

Bud thinks there are twice as many tourists this year and it will be worse with the new ferry next year. We agree that's terrible. I can complain. I'm not a "tourist." I'm "summer people," since I've been coming here long enough to have childhood memories of the place and since our family refuses to sell off the little strip of woods we own, though we don't lack offers. It's our small act of island preservation. We come here for the pleasure of repetition, regular as rising and falling tides.

Most people come here once. The worst come for a day, drive the length of the island, sleep over, notch their belts, and head north to bag Prince Edward and Cape Breton. It takes years to properly visit the place. To know which bog ponds are good for skinny-dipping, where the wild blueberries ripen earliest, where the first gooseberries and the last wild raspberries. It takes years to notice a singular gull—one that dives like a cormorant, showing an evolutionary anomaly that may change the future of its species, or the fool gull so aggressive it never eats, constantly chasing its flockmates away from the feast of a seine drawn on shore to be cleaned and repaired. It takes years of lying still on the bluff at Swallowtail to know that tourists come, wonder briefly over the view, and go. It's not worth the effort of feeling invaded. The island is like poetry: most people don't have time for it.

Before we had the cottage, we stayed at an inn called Rose Cottage, where several families took room and board. We ate in a big old-fashioned dining room with tablecloths, homemade rolls, and a crank-up telephone. A family from Toronto had a daughter my age and son my brother's. We kids could walk anywhere—down the road or the trails—and islanders treated us like something special, inviting us in for a handful of crispy dulse. Evenings we'd run like wildcats through the hallways until it was time to settle on the floor beside a stove-size radio through which we strained to hear episodes of *Boston Blackie*. There were outings to remote islands, lobster parties on the beach, and hikes to the Hole in the Wall, the Southern Cross, the Flock of Sheep—formations of rock that on the California coast would be so commonplace as to go unnoticed. Here each was singular and worthy of pilgrimage.

We too had our singular status, as summer people, and as Americans. Everyone knew our names and told stories about the things we'd done together last summer. Our cachet increased with adolescence, the sexual economy being defined by limited supply and exaggerated demand. There were wild, scary teenage times—the flip side of the island's religious propriety and repression. In the fifties, liquor wasn't sold and drinking was considered immoral. Our parents would place an order with the purser on the ferry, who brought back the precious bottles from the mainland for the ritual cocktail hour. The islanders, in response to the prohibition, drank in the binge-and-purge style, tumbling into fierce bouts of booze when it was available. Teenagers made home brew out of grape juice and got sickly drunk at beach parties and backwoods deer camps. My brother ran with a wild crowd, managed to convince the parents that it was legal in Canada for a sixteen-year-old to drive without a license. He and his buddies careened for weeks, wrecked a car or two before the Mountie caught up with him.

Sex had the same trigger-happy danger to it. By thirteen the guys were randy and ready to go, quickly gearing up into a passion that was all horsepower and no brakes. For the girls it was different. Scared and aroused, we'd play the edges of desire until we came to a boundary we weren't ready to cross. One time some half-lit men picked up my friend and me to give us a ride home. One took me in the back seat and the others said, "Give her a hickey!" I didn't know what it was, only that it was bad for a girl to get one and that they thought it was funny to try. I felt the danger then, and later with guys I dated—men who I knew could force themselves on a woman. But there were others who would take you to see the sunset night after night, and together you'd watch the boundary between day and night melt away.

August 6

Sunday. Rain. From the table I watch the ferry float in through the fog like a celestial ship through a cloud, its foghorn sounding the way to port. The point where Swallowtail perches has melted into white, and the music of rain—percussion, woodwind, reed—plays through the cottage. Rain beads on the freshly painted deck outside my window. I find it a pleasure to catch up with the disrepair —nature's disregard for human beings—manifest in the moss growing on cross-members of the deck rail, moisture lifting paint in flakes off the railing, window trims, and door. Every two years the deck needs repainting; fifteen years and the roof gets reshingled. These are the facts. Language and reflection answer facts the way repair answers disrepair. Paint seals the surface of wood— the old stuff drinking in the thick liquid until its surface cells are too full to take in the sea mist and the rain.

August 10

White Head, again. This time with Garry, who's come from his summer workplace on Swan's Island, Maine. It's always special to have a first-time visitor to the island, touring with him the remote landmarks: Dark Harbour, Beech Hill, Seal Cove Beach, Hay Point—places with names that describe them. And the visitors are duly impressed. Twice when my parents brought friends here for a weekend, they left owning a house. (That was when the houses cost less than an economy car.) The only friends who bother coming up here are ones charmed by the discomforts—no reservations for the ferry, no swimmable beaches, no bars or resorts, a network of trails fit primarily for sheep, the occasional scent of wild roses, the more common and rank perfume of smoked herring as the road descends into one quaint village or another.

Garry and I walk the gravel road back to the bog pond. Someone has left a dinghy with oars on a patch of marsh grass. No one in sight. Why leave the oars if the owner doesn't want others to take the boat across? On the far side we find a slapdash bench—just a bunch of driftwood lumber stacked up on a small sphagnum peninsula. We sit, take turns casting the copper wobbler into the circles that ripple out and intersect on the tea-dark surface. Whatever is feeding isn't interested in our bait, but we stay and talk about islands, nature, and God.

He's lived in Hawaii, traveled islands of the South Pacific, and tells how Jehovah's Witnesses propagated their seed on one tropical island, how the natives would dress up in Western clothes to go to church. Up here it seems the smaller the island, the more churches thrive on it. The people are susceptible, he says, because of their isolation. Yes, and they're opened to omnipotence by their exposure to ocean and sky. The danger of working at sea.

The cattails glisten and sway, silver-edged in the sun, their brown torches leaning slightly into the north. We talk about his growing up in Florida, where children regularly drowned or died of snakebite. Swimming in a bog pond would have meant risking an encounter with water moccasins. Here in the north not much in nature is dangerous—a few mushrooms and spiders whose scale and scarcity are such that they don't make a child afraid to go out. Yet fishermen die here every winter, as one of them told us—a man we met one evening at the Whistle who had brought his mother to watch the sunset. His last time, the boat was out for forty-two straight hours, weather tipping the vessel so you could walk up its sides. It filled with waves. There was nothing to do but ride out the storm ... and, in his case, quit fishing.

A friend, Stanley Small, lost his arm in a wringer while fishing one winter off Sable Island. Nine men in a boat, stuck in the ice for five days—he said they'd laugh one minute and cry the next, and weren't ashamed to say so. Quitting, even for him, wasn't easy. He saw things out there he couldn't believe. A phalanx of whales migrating, cruising the surface side by side; you could have stepped off the boat and walked a mile on their backs, he said, if you could stand the stench of their blowholes. Porpoises, column after column, a mile and a half long, arcing and diving in unison like a synchronized halftime show. Dolphins hitching rides for two days by resting their tails against the bow. How many men did he know who were lost at sea? He'd stopped counting at fifty-eight.

The wind has come up. The bog pond is choppy, and we row into gusts that want to drift us down into the cattail rushes. G. sizes up the resistance, redirects the boat into the lee, and rows us in a parabolic curve around the sheltered shore. I love that he understands the water, wind, and currents, taking the long way around to make things easy. Others would try to plough straight through, fighting the obvious all the way. But he's a painter and he's used to looking for what others haven't seen.

AUGUST 12
Saturday. 6 P.M. The fishermen's wharf. A seiner chugs out toward Long Island. A swarm of small seabirds races back and forth six inches over the water, scanning for feed. A pickup rips down to the end of the wharf, speakers blasting. A party beginning, it looks like, on a purse seiner named Rolling Stone. Four other teenagers sit in a subcompact car and circle a joint. Down in the green kelp-ridden harbor, along the creosote pilings of the breakwater, beer

bottles bob and herring or tinker mackerel meander. Saturday night begins, and all night I'll hear the scream of cars, the bass line of cassette players booming down the road. It's how our young claim their piece of adulthood—with noise and wildness and speed. How many years of it before they'll be attending a church supper on Saturday nights—Baptist or Wesleyan for the populists, Anglican for the elite?

AUGUST 13
I wake up dreaming of riding horses with my daughter. Sunday. Another dazzling day. Thinking of nature and young women, their bodies commandeered by reproductive chemistry before they realize they're sexual beings, their need to feel the harmony and power of their relationship with nature. In the sun-slick ocean this morning, over east, I see a smudge. As it approaches, a shape. It looks like a tugboat hauling a smokestacked crate. Not until it's even with the bell buoy at Swallowtail does it turn broadside so that I see its size: an oil tanker or barge. Might as well carry a plague flag from its masthead. This is the summer the Exxon *Valdez* stepped up the course of evolution in Alaska. If that had happened here, the island would be finished. People wouldn't be able to fish for ten years. The cliffs would be slimed with black oil, carcasses battered into the rocks. And just yesterday some of us were proud to claim that oil tankers don't come into the Bay of Fundy. What is it doing here? A ship in trouble? Great. It lumbers, with its prehistoric cargo, toward port.

I drive down to the wharf to find out it's only the *Irving Seal*— a small tanker, maybe fifteen car lengths—making its regular benign delivery of fuel to the island. The tug maneuvers the steel hulk up to the breakwater. A tug has always seemed to me a friendly boat, stout and tough like a workhorse. This one sports a yellow-and-black stack, kelly green railings, Canadian and corporate flags. She breathes hard and deep, puffs black, nestles the behemoth into her berth. A winch swings out to the pier, men wrench open the pipeline that runs along it up to the white storage tanks on the hill. The first thing you see when the ferry slides into port is that cluster of giant fuel tanks. I never thought before how much depends on them, by what risks the island has earned its comforts. An umbilicus is hoisted over, clamped on and the island takes its nutrient.

A purse seiner dawdles into port, riding low, its hold full of pollock and cod. Out on the intertidal zone an old rusted storage tank catches my eye. I think I see a grubby long-hair crouched there, leaning to take in the morning news. It's just a tire and some rockweed, though it became for a moment an apparition of the kid who two years ago paddled a canoe out into the riptide, he and his buddy both ripped for the Saturday revels, and didn't come back.

AUGUST 18
Last hike of the summer. The trail to Indian Beach edges a precipitous wall of basalt several hundred feet high, volcanic rocks crumbling down to rubble at the base, leveling off to a beach of rounded stones heaped with drifted logs. The woods are dense. Blackberry canes arch over the trail. I eat a handful of the juicy explosions, gather more along the way. The island is fifteen miles long and five wide, its western side inaccessible from the water except by a wooden dory, which is sturdy enough to grind up onto the stone beaches. One dirt road cuts across to Dark Harbour, the only substantial break in the massive wall that makes up the western side. Legend has it that even the native people who paddled over from the mainland found the island bleak and inhospitable, suitable only for foraging gull eggs and gathering eels. Their name for it, according to one historian, was Munanouk, meaning *sea island* as distinguished from lake island, river island, or hill island. The same inconsequential name applied to a number of islands off the North Atlantic coast.

Someone has released pheasants and wild turkeys to roam and multiply in these woods, but I don't encounter them today. Forty years ago the men had hunts on the island—so many points for an eagle, crow, crane. It was sport. A guy would come grinning out of the backwoods—See what I've got—with the birds dangling from his belt by their claws. I overheard one of the old-timers tell the story—and this: not one of them today wouldn't want to live it again. Not one of them that doesn't regret what he did.

The woods are active with breezes and bees, fields of maidenhair ferns, red squirrels shinnying in and out of a hollow pine. The chuff of a deer's heavy breathing as it leaps out of harm's way. Giant beech trees—the climax species—each claiming a wide circle of the sparse forest light, starving out the alders or spruce that might start below. How these beings live, what they perceive, what this landscape has learned of geology and natural history, I can't know. I strain to fathom the place, as if it has an awareness of its own to convey that will settle somewhere like seeds in my consciousness, feeding me when I'm sickened with despair at the limits of my own nature or those I love.

The cliff softens, the trail switchbacks down to Indian Beach, where a few dulse shacks are planted on coarse stones. Nets stretch out for drying the purple weed on the heated stones. Spiders race in and out of the interstices, another unlikely niche inhabited by entrepreneurial creatures. The spines of an old weir stand the watch offshore. It's not solitude I experience when alone here, but connectedness—the seawater that links continents and inconsequential islands, the seawater working in all living cells.

AUGUST 20

My last afternoon. I walk down to the stone beach across the road in front of the cottage. Dozens of blue-spangled dragonflies: do they migrate like butterflies or go dormant in the cold? Rocks worn so that their history is bald—a red one streuseled with lime green, a tawny neapolitan, black ones etched with precise white lines, a lightweight fist of motley lava, purple rocks smooth as plums. This time I walk south where the stones get bigger, grapefruit-sized, but don't cease to be miraculous—conglomerates of purple and turquoise, swirls of pink and gray, some baked with nuggets of green. No matter how many times I've been down here, I still find a half-dozen rocks unlike any other I've seen, and I have to lug the things up the hill to marvel over. That painter who makes the hyper-real rocks—I think that his paintings, as true as they are, are a lie. Because that work was done by nature, the forge of the elements subjected to pressure and heat, *that* work has already been done and his mere copying, though accurate, is slight. The wonder is that these things exist with no help from the human hand. I gather a bowlful as if they are fruit. The annual harvest.

Sunlight fractures through the broken clouds, local shafts singling out first the lighthouse, then the lumpy cliff where it sits, next the yellow Anglican church in the village, then humps of rockweed-covered boulders, then the makeshift bench where I sit. That lava. The melted, layered, folded rocks. Interbedded sedimentary strata. A fault line cuts through the Castalia Bank nearby, exposing the most varied rocks on the island. They make the earth appear young and in process. Is the land still rising up from the earth's viscous mantle? Rising up from beneath more slowly than it wears down from above? Or is this a settled topography revealing more of its history than its process—as a person's face tells a history. I'm thinking of a woman, superficially religious, who has aged with torment grained into her. She suffered two abusive, alcoholic husbands, both of whom died prematurely. She believes her reward will be in the hereafter, and that the degree to which she suffers in life will set the measure of her bliss to come, so she wears her anguish with pride. I know a man whose face shows the lines of happiness with which he wakes every morning, whether he has slept poorly or hasn't a dollar to his name. Or myself, whose emerging age lines are a squint between the eyebrows and the bridge of the nose, because I keep straining to see things more clearly. That's how history is made, right down to the brain cells that physically change to incorporate a new memory—part of the process of shaping and holding that all nature practices.

I have located myself for another year. Coming back here satisfies the part of me that's ancient, some shred of stuff in me that's been handed down from one DNA strand to another for eons, descended from the migratory flocks and tribes who knew how to read the planet without a map. The seal's head I've been noticing for hours again slips out of the water to watch me. I click and call, and it seems to respond with its attention. Maybe if I sit here every day it will come closer. More likely we'll both wander off to inspect something new and more interesting. Few creatures have the patience to try to tame a human being.

THE PERFECT HIKE

NO SIGN MARKS THE TRAILHEAD—JUST A BEND IN
the road, a dent in the bordering alders and blackberry canes. I've
never taken this trail so early in summer. Usually I wait for the
berries to ripen so that I can snack along the way on my excursion
into solitude. This time the white cumulus of blossoms rains pollen
and petals on my head as I pass underneath and enter the roadless
wilds of the island's backside. The power line cuts through here, a
scar fifty yards wide running parallel to the road, healing now
where alders have staked their claim. They are the reclamation
species in this part of the world—the first brush to grow back after
bulldozers and backhoes have reduced green to brown. I head
downhill toward the cliff edge, scouting for the trail marker to
Indian Beach.

I have longed for this hike, arriving on Grand Manan this year
after a cross-country flight from my home in Tucson, after driving
my mother from her home in Connecticut up the Maine coast and
into New Brunswick, after arriving on the last ferry of the day to
find that a winter job of repairing a rotten sill beam had left our
cottage looking like a trashed backwoods deer camp. Sixteen years
of gravity and fog had worked on the decaying wood to give our
bathroom a lean that made the tub impossible to drain without
bailing pooled water from the deep end up to the drain hole. Since
my father's death two years ago, my mother has learned more than
she ever hoped to know about home maintenance. And she has had
to learn it without much money or experience negotiating with

contractors. My father's Yankee thrift and pride in self-sufficiency had meant that disrepair tended to remain invisible to him. When he died he left us with two beloved houses sagging in neglect. In the first year my mother had to replace the roof, the water heater, the electric stove, the bathroom floor, and several hot-spots of electrical wiring in the Connecticut house. On Grand Manan, after overseeing repairs on the perpetually leaking roof and the perpetually inadequate well-water supply, she conceded at my urging that the bathroom's back wall had sunken finally too low. We imagined all winter how wonderful it would be to see that long slow slump corrected—one more fear about the lifespan of our ramshackle part-time home allayed. We had fidgeted in the dark through the padlocks on the shed and kitchen doors, flipped the fuse box, pulled the light-chain and were greeted by domestic doom. A shambles of scrap sheetrock, limp and soggy from a winter's worth of fog, hunks of discarded copper pipe and fittings, a paint-splattered plywood floor laid in the "new" bathroom, the toilet seeping Rorschachs from a broken seal onto the raw thirsty floor, buckets of rags and slime, fuses blown, molded shower curtain tossed in a stiffened heap. My mother was ready to plough the house down, sell off our few precious acres of woods and start from scratch. The workmen of course had just laughed, jovially blaming us for arriving too soon. After a week of frantic dumping, scrubbing, spackling, and painting, my mother and I began to talk as usual about how much we loved this shambled place. And I set my sights on the woods.

Twenty minutes in, the rhythm of walking has comfortably loosened my muscles and joints. I'm moving like the animal I am, instead of the awkward, stiffened city version of myself that never feels at home on a sidewalk or a bus. Up an incline I come to a clearing in the spruce where a granite dome breaks through the forest floor. Most of the rock mass is buried, but this forehead of stone lies bare. Some gray reindeer moss, yellow lichen, and a green mat of moss have worked at covering the rock, and in spots have succeeded. Tasseled timothy grows out of the cracks and bowls where humus has had years to thicken, years to catch random airborne seeds so they could settle into the moist soil, germinate, spring forth from the tangle of roots that now cements soil to rock. This past spring has been richly wet—that's apparent from the meatiness of the trees' new growth. A scrim of tall plush spruce and slender new-leaved birch separates me from the cliff. The boggy ground resilient as a wet sponge. Last year the woods were so dry that even this peat-thick soil began to look like tinder and the trees grew scrawny and desperate.

The Indian Beach Trail follows the cliffline along the uninhabited western side of the island. The pleasure of this trail is that one simultaneously experiences the enclosure of deep forest and the expansiveness of open sea. Sitting to rest and make notes, I hear a vigorous flapping rise up from the ocean, which eddies and laps four hundred feet below. From this leafy vantage, it's hard to tell whether the ruckus comes from terns or whitecaps. Both perhaps—a windy sunny day, that hair-brushing music of wind zithering through delicate birches. The silence that brings such sounds to my attention is why I come here. This gentleness, this refinement of perception gets lost in the thick-skinned compromises of professional life, the conflicts between my responsibilities to others and my need to hold this solitary conversation with the pure sensuality of experience. I come year after year to this wild island because here my mind feels free, in love with being, with place, sensation, blue sky, green, more green, and sunlight sharpening the waxy spindles on the rain-happy spruce.

James Hillman says that the experience of beauty is now the unconscious, in the sense that the unconscious, rather than being a bedlam of hidden monstrosities held captive in the dark cells of the brain, is whatever we're not currently conscious of. William Wordsworth, another enthusiast of walking, found that his most desired state of mind could be induced only in a "round of strenuous idleness." His daffodils persisted not merely as things of beauty, but because he understood how they filled an absence in the mind that craved them. When alone in the woods, I trust my mind, accept its insistence on counterpoint, the rapid shape-shifting between what is conscious, what is unconscious. I think this must be the animal way of mind—not willing certain thoughts, but being had by them, following them like scent.

I hear a sail luffing below and remember how shocked I was to arrive this year and see seven yachts moored in the harbor beside the herring boats—unusual for these treacherous waters, a working island. On the ferry I was dismayed to see a rack of brochures advertising new rental cottages, sea kayaking, and whale-watching tours. The provincial government is investing in ecotourism, since the Bay of Fundy is at risk of losing its fisheries. Haddock is already difficult to find at the fish stands. They're nearly fished out in these waters, as some fear the herring are. Newfoundland's cod fishery has been closed down by the government for two years, the fishermen learning to live on unemployment insurance. Cod!—the fish for which New England was settled and a prominent part of it named—reduced from fat harvest to a former job.

The sound of heavy sails whacks in the wind.

What a clear, deep green the water is when seen from the clifftop, translucent manes of kelp blowing in the water as if in wind. I've come to a lookout where the trail meets the drop-off, a patch of worn grass where other walkers have lingered to watch the riptides tatter the Channel's surface. Hundreds of seabirds float in a scattered mass a hundred yards offshore. I don't know if they are terns, gulls, or gannets. A few take off, their angular lean wings like boomerangs against the sky. Whatever they are, they prefer water to land. There are pelagic species—shearwater, petrel, fulmar—that come to land only during breeding season and then only under cover of darkness. Nevertheless, their useful properties have not gone undiscovered. Storm petrels, my Audubon field guide reports, because of their high oil content "were at one time used as lamps. A cotton wick was inserted in the throat of a dead bird,

which when lighted would burn for a considerable length of time."
A wave of excitement passes through the seabirds gathered down
there, their voices rising like a stadium full of cheering fans.

Despite my fear for the privacy of this place, I haven't seen one
kayak in the Bay, no lines of photo-snapping tourists, no guided
tours of the woods—in fact, I haven't seen a single person on the
trail all morning. Better yet, the closer I get to Indian Beach, the
more poorly maintained the trail becomes. By the time I reach Eel
Brook, where the passage of water has softened the cliffline to a
steep though negotiable slope, there's no trail at all. The incline is
nearly vertical, dropping through the scraggly woods that hold
most of the slope in place. No sign of footfalls or trailblazes—a
mere ghost of a trail where a few prior walkers made an approxi-
mation of the best way down. No prints except a deer's weaving—
it also couldn't decide on the best route down. Hurray for the
desolate, the rugged, the crude, which keep people away from this
place of solitude.

Time for a sturdy walking stick. Time to test my Vibram soles.
Another year's wear and tear on the body—not quite the strength
in the ankles or knees I had twenty years ago, when I first skidded
giggling down this incline. I can do this, I insist when my boots slip
on scree. Just need to slow down. Not ready for years to give up
this trail, though a bone-breaking fall down this hillside miles into
the woods would be an adventure. No means of rescue but a dulse-
picker's dory, if I were lucky enough to find one on the beach. And
who would know where to look for me? Slow down, grip spruce
boughs, test roots to see what holds firm.

While I'm having this cautionary conversation with myself, I
realize that my note taking means that I'm making this hike not
only for myself, but perhaps for someone who can no longer
walk—or someone who never walked—someone sucking ice chips
in the birthing room, someone stuck on minimum wage, someone
jailed or dying. I began thinking this way about hiking during the
year and a half of my father's decline when he suffered a heart

attack, two strokes, Legionnaires' disease, and finally a tortured institutional death. I began thinking of him whenever I was in the woods, knowing how much he loved to walk dwarfed beneath hickories or beeches, and knowing that he would not enter woods again. I stopped thinking about men who machete their way through Borneo, and I began to carry my father's spirit on my walks.

After skidding down the slope, I climb over the berm and onto Indian Beach—a desolate cobble of flattened gray rocks. Each beach on the island has its characteristic geomorphisms—black sand at Deep Cove, polished plum-colored spheres on the Castalia Bank, the white quartz and green rhyolites of Bancroft Point. Here a deep, shifting rubble of dull ovals (basalt eroded from the cliffs?) has piled up, making a beach that clatters underfoot. A huge windrow of drifted timbers has collected at the high-tide line— scrap, slat, beam, uprooted trees, hulls, and rafters—all beached and bleached the same gray. No beachcombers here. Dropping down a ridge of stones taller than myself to get to the waterline, I kick the cobble loose and ride the gravel wave to level ground. At water's edge the stones are smaller and with each outflowing wave they make a sound like clacking marbles. The water's surface is marked with rip currents that make this passage famous for ship-wrecks—whorls and glass-flat pools, meandering rivers of torque moving between fluid banks of calm. There are six dulse shacks scattered along Indian Beach—one tar paper, two weathered cedar shingle, two weathered plywood, one eight-by-ten prefab log cabin—and two outhouses. Dulse nets are spread out on the rocks, the heat of which on a good day will hasten the drying of the har-vested purple seaweed. Today the nets lie empty.

A weir stands offshore. I'm always happy to see a weir, both for the art of its construction and for the way of life it represents. Weirs are built for catching herring. In older times the fish were cured and smoked at fish stands right on Grand Manan, packed in wooden cases and shipped to market. Now a few smokehouses operate, but most herring are hauled by carrier boat to the sardine factory in Blacks Harbour. This weir, standing a hundred feet off-shore, is anchored with a steel cable to the boulders at the cliff's base. A vertical net, standing from the ocean bed to the water's surface, runs from the shoreline out to the weir's open mouth, then curves to form a heart-shaped enclosure. Schools of herring, chased shoreward by pollock and hake, run into the netted twine and divert their course into the weir. Once inside the structure, the fish tend to circle and to lose track of the way out. Cedar or balsam stakes make the weir's frame, birch saplings spliced onto them for rigging the twine. The lumber is not milled, but rough-cut with a chainsaw. The twine laced onto the structure droops slightly between stakes to give the weir's upper edge a graceful scalloped line. When the weir fills with herring, a pumper boat comes out, slips inside and men drop the purse seine to gather the catch. From shore the twine looks translucent. I don't see the strands in the twine's weave, but a gray haze hanging on the wooden frame, a darkening of that hue where I look through two or three thick-nesses of netting. My eyesight shifts toward a finer grain of seeing as I linger in the pleasure of the weir's rough-hewn order, its imper-fect handmade geometry.

Black spiders two inches wide flit in and out of the stones under my perch on a battered gray beam. They appear, disappear with hyperactive regularity, scooting down the little tunnels between rounded stones. There seems to be no demarcation for them between above- and below-ground. They've never bitten me in all the times I've sat among them to eat my picnic lunch—today, a lentil sandwich with red oakleaf lettuce and arugula from Al Hobbs's garden. I kill spiders indoors I admit. And my mother sprays Raid to mark a boundary around her bed because last year she was bitten on the toe and couldn't play tennis for a week. She blamed a fit of chills and shaking on the bite. I almost didn't make my scheduled departure—her first time here alone since my father's death—fearing a stroke was coming on. But out here the spiders don't frighten me. Someday I'll learn they're brown recluse spiders, the most lethal of our domestic companions—but I doubt it. They seem so uninterested in flesh, scurrying about this Mars of boulder and stone. I imagine they eat the fleas that stick to mats of washed-up kelp and rockweed. Slim pickings, no matter what they go for. Thirty yards back from the beach lies a meadow of grass, wild-flowers, and bugs. But the spiders shun that wasteland for this monochromatic bounty of stone.

The tide's going out. I think I can avoid going up that butt-slider of a trail by following the boulder beach south to Money Cove. I cross my fingers that the way up to the cliff trail is better there, or at least identifiable from shore. I'm heading farther away from habitations, even from the dulsing ground. The only route from this point on is the beach. Eventually, I will need to climb back into the island's midsection and cut east across the woods to the road. And if I can't find the trail? Four choices—be stuck here all night, backtrack, bushwhack, or flag down a boat. It has been three hours since that wing-flapping yacht passed out of earshot. Not a working boat in sight all day. As for bushwhacking, it's not too effective through the island's soggy interior of bog ponds and marshes. There will be no backtracking, because by the time I make it to the next inset cove, the tide will have closed the gap between the cliff and the shore. Assessing the risks, I go on, excited by the tension of not knowing what lies ahead.

If Indian Beach was a rubble, then the beach leading to Money Cove is a ruin—a mountain of drifted bleached timber, fallen shacks, leaning shacks, a rusted winch that must once have hauled dories onto the beach, mattress springs, bird-pillaged mattress stuffing, algae-coated heaps of broken glass, a rusted frypan, a wood cookstove sprung apart into its component panels and disks, rotten ropes and floats and ripped-up twine—all jumbled into the visual harmony of being long-worn. This is old garbage, and old garbage is clean.

I'm soaked with sweat from the hard walk and ahead stretches a minefield—a rocky intertidal zone covered with green slimeweed. I test the birch walking stick—a stout one so fresh it hasn't lost the bark. Crossing this ground is like walking in stockings across silk. I rest halfway, near the ruin of an old stone sluiceway used for torching herring. Triangular wooden frames tall as a house hold back the rocks from the sluiceway, which leads from the sea to a hand-built seawater pond. At night the fishermen used to shine torches on the water, attracting herring into the pond. This one has been long in disuse; the pond is algal wastewater.

The sky's beginning to look like rain and I begin to wonder just how far down the beach Money Cove is. I haven't come this far down the island's backside before, though my first short story, written in ninth grade, took place here. It was an imitation of one I'd read—one of those insipid children's stories that try to allay fear by explaining the mystery out of a mysterious situation. I didn't know enough about the power of an open-ended story to leave well enough alone. Its only strength was the island legend it drew upon: a pirate ship had gone down off the coast not long after its captain had buried his loot near these cliffs, and on the anniversary of his death, a ghost ship was seen passing by the cove, turning and passing again as the destitute spirit searched for his gold. I slapped a contemporary frame on the story—an adventuresome little girl wants more than anything to see the apparition, so on the appointed night she camps out on the beach to bear witness and, to her amazement and delectable fear, the ship appears at midnight; later the truth comes out that her sadistic older brother has merely created the illusion of the ghost ship to scare her. Even at that age, I knew I had wimped out by making the world a safe place where deception replaces the essential mysteries: death, transmutation, a treasure outlasting the grave.

The importance of story on the island is that it creates a common language. "Well, I'm going to pull an Ed Young on you," Lester said after we found the scale baskets in my cellar so that I could collect the scrap shingles he'd pulled loose from the eaves.

"What's that?" I asked, knowing I was about to be let in on a local confidence. "Oh," he said, egging me on, "you never heard that story?" "I don't think so." "Well, you see, Ed Young was riding Megs down the big hill there by Seal Cove when the chain came off the bicycle. And so he says to her, 'Here's where I get off, Megs.' Can you imagine saying that? And she was riding on the handlebars. So he jumps off, rolls over, breaks his arm and stuff. But Megs, she just rolled down the hill onto a big soft lawn. Well, there's justice for you. And that's where the saying comes from ... 'Here's where I get off, Megs.' I don't know if it was true," Lester chuckled, "but it makes a good story."

A quarter mile down the shore I see that the cliff dips gradually toward the beach, the shoreline indenting to form what appears to be a cove—another twenty minutes' walk ahead on this tidal wave of shifting stones. With no trail markers and no map except the one in my head, all I can read is that cliffline, that dents into the woods. I head on, trusting that others who have come here will have left some sign of the best way out. If all else fails, I'll spend the night huddled under boughs. Part of me wants that honest hardship, wants to know that, if necessary, I could survive on roots and birds and rain.

Money Cove is the first soft place I've seen all day. A sloping wall of the flattened oval stones piled by waves has closed the cove from the sea. Where once a small vessel might have found shelter, now a grassy marsh has spread its claim. A clear meandering stream cuts through the narrow meadow—broad-bladed marsh grasses, blue flag, cattails, and reeds. The marsh melts gradually back into the woods. On the higher ground grows a thicket of wild raspberry canes.

I'm not the first one to read the cliff and end in this spot. A grassy trail heads up the marsh bank inland toward the woods. Just up the rise stands a half-built shack of beach scrap and tar paper. It has no door so I step in. There are two picture windows—one facing the marsh, the other the beach and a weir staked offshore.

On the marsh side, strewn down the weedy slope, are broken liquor bottles and mildewed playing cards. The inside is neat and spare—a banged-up wooden dining table, the top painted, legs mottled green, set beside the front window; a shallow rectangular kitchen sink though there's no running water or drain; three dinner plates stacked on the shelf under the sink; above, mismatched mugs and jelly glasses. The floor has been swept—a haggard broom leans in the corner beside a hammer and crowbar. Triple bunks, no mattresses, the topmost tier a foot from the ceiling—fit for a small child. The place may be makeshift, but it's well loved, if creating domestic order is a measure of love.

A pile of bird scat on the otherwise tidy floor. Above, a mud-wattled nest glued to the rafter, three barn swallows, which don't budge though I'm three feet from their nervous heads. Their terror of me is palpable, yet they do not cry out in fear or warning, or leave the nest where eggs must be warming under their down-covered breasts. For them it appears that protecting their genetic heritage is more important than personal safety. Their courage sends me back out the door.

Why do I love the barren, the desolate? The shack with its yard trimmed free of weeds to encourage daisies and wild currants. The damaged beauty of the littered beach, picked over by people, ravens, and gulls. Why should this experience make me so happy? Why should it please me that waste and ruin are not hidden here, while in the city—the same being true—I can't kick myself free of elegy. Here there is no fashion, no vanity, no empire, no art but that of making do. People's lives are one part of a continuous song for several voices that the gulls, the sea, the eroding cliffs of basalt, the sieving beach cobble, the crinkling page, and the rising breeze are singing. Suffering dissolves into the liquid day.

A few paces up the steep trail out I find an ATV track and the faded blue trailblazes I'd hoped for. They lead me into beech forest, the high crowning trees opening beneath them a meadow of maidenhair ferns. Sunlight filigrees down through the leaves. I've seen so many favorite sights today that endorphins are coloring my mood like a dazzling sunset. And the day's not over yet. In the hollow of a fallen tree—the stump upright and open like a lidless oil barrel—lying on a bed of densely packed wood rot is a heap of bird bones, one bone nearly twice as long as a drumstick, and a few scrappy feathers that have lost their silk. At first I think it's a nest, but nothing has lain on this scatter of desiccated feathers and bone for years. It has taken on a pale algal hue from dwelling in the moist hold of the stump. Was it a raven? eagle? wild turkey? Impossible to tell from the evidence. I don't touch the jumble—it looks too much like a grave, something ritual about the layout that I don't want to disturb.

The trail snakes around a series of bog ponds and swamps, heading east, then south. I've been lost crossing the island's soggy midsection before and soon realize that I will again have trouble with the forest. At least the sun has returned as a guide. I've lost the hatchmarks of the blue trail and now follow one of several ATV tracks. Worse, I slowly come to notice that for ten minutes I've been slogging back into the sun—not a good idea when I'm trying to head east in late afternoon. By the time I cross a stream for the third time, I know I'm in trouble—two ponds have been on my left, now one on my right. I try to read the topographical map in my mind, but where I stand can't be the shore of either Little Lake or Eel Lake—just an etched out area on the map that's a bog in dry years and a pond when it's wet. How much I long to strip down and slip into the water—sweating and worn from six hours on foot—but the shore is all slop and mire. The best I can do is admire the iridescent dragonflies whose veined wings gleam and tremble over the water—and taste the bog pond's spillover with my feet and ankles, the icy water a salve.

A bird startles noisily and cruises over the pond—nearly as large as an eagle, mottled brown and white. It perches on top of a dead spruce at the far end of the water and watches me pass. Probably an osprey, but I'm too tired to stop and pull binoculars out of my

pack. Then—eureka!—a wild strawberry in my path. Sixth one of
the day I've found in a wild pool of sunlight, the fruit tiny and hot,
perfectly ripe. Six strawberries. A good day's pay.

I come to a logging site, slag scattered in a rough clearing, tire
tracks leading off in at least four directions. I'm totally disoriented
from the network of ponds I've been circling for the last two hours.
The only homemade instructions I can cook up are to take the
widest road and to keep the sun on my back. I invoke the logic of
rivers—tributaries join and head for the sea. Backwoods trails join,
everyone eventually heading back home. And on this island, everyone's home lies east of the woods. Up until now I've been counting the day's wonders like syllables in a literalist's mantra—cliff
birch kelp tern spiders rubble cove marsh swallows ferns beeches
bone-tree berries. But now I'm exhausted, legs gone, and the sun's
flirting with a menacing bank of cloud.

I follow one of the tracks made by a skidder, pass a dead van
rigged for a hunting camp, antlers strapped to the rearview mirror,
then a camp with door ajar revealing dropleaf gunports for a
hunter who likes his comforts; come to a four-corners where I have
to choose between widest road and sun on my back. I take the road
most traveled, slog on, and still I'm nowhere. I fear if I stop my leg
muscles will freeze, the ache bone-deep in my hips, thighs, and feet.
One last time I slide my back down the trunk of a fat tree, lean into
its coolness, and let myself slow down. All I need is a blue blaze,
all I need is to recross the power line. All I need is to see one famil-
iar stretch of ground. But when I do find the power line, on its far
side lie more woods, ahead no sight of the road, no distant hum-
ming of cars. I start to think that even here on this tame wild
island, its topography imprinted like a storybook in my brain, I
could become hopelessly lost. Being slightly lost is one pleasure of
hiking here—trying an unmarked way, trusting my ability to read
the terrain, and having my trust rewarded. How foolish I would
feel admitting to the deer hunters that I'd had to spend the night
shivering on damp ground.

I suppose it is the sight, smell, or sound of metal that warns an animal of human presence—as well as the onion scent of our sweat. It's metal that welcomes me back to the fold—the trail butting a deer-proof fence closing off a ten-acre stand of dwarf apple trees. I slip the metal catch, swing the gate open, and stand ecstatic within the order of a humanized environment, columns and rows of nurtured trees, young trunks wrapped in protective plastic, diminutive crowns glowing green. Downhill past the far gate of the orchard, a glimpse through woods—a car whizzes by. I'm rid of all need but home.

Jacquetta Hawkes in her natural history of the British Isles, *A Land,* writes that perception alters not only the past but landscape itself, and that landscape in turn shapes consciousness. This is what I come here for—to make the place a part of me, to make myself this place. Silent glide of flight with nothing to say but flight, sheep laurel blooming in acid shade, the lure of hiking deeper into the wilds, endlessly hungry, endlessly fed—"Beautiful my desire," Roethke wrote, "and the place of my desire." Every year when I leave this island I weep, as if I were leaving a lover I can't bear to leave. I watch the cliffs recede behind the ferry's green-and-white churn and I feel a part of myself being ripped out. In that moment when the eros of place pulls on me, I begin to write—words being the only way to invite this lover inside.

SIDECUTS

THIRD DAY OF FOG. I SIT AT THE WOODEN DINING
table my parents bought in 1958 on Long Island, a one-mile-long
bump of land now uninhabited that sits in the Bay's muffled sog
just east of our cottage on Grand Manan. They hauled a houseload
of stuff over here on a fishing boat—potato crates fashioned into
end tables, iron bed frames, a few sturdy oak pieces, pine bureaus
with hand-painted black curlicues and pin-striping and built-on
wooden candle sconces. The family who'd lived out there ended
badly. There was talk of drink and fighting, dishes smashed
throughout the house.

Our cottage was built in 1864. A family of seven lived here year-
round—mother and father, four children, and an uncle. The kids
slept lined up in one bed head-to-toe like sardines. Someone told
me that a man who lived here had barely survived when his ship
went down off Nova Scotia. He spent nine days adrift in a dory
with a jar of water, then moved to Grand Manan. I think he was
the one who built this house on the Castalia Bank. The only insulation a layer of birchbark laid between the planking and the
plaster. No running water—a hand pump in a trough in the
kitchen. No electricity. Two wood stoves—one for cooking and
one for heat.

We ploughed down the outhouse, piped in water from a spring
on the hill, and spread spackle with a shingle to patch the crumbling interior walls. Only my mother's insistence and her small
inheritance from a librarian she'd befriended at their first home in

Wethersfield, Connecticut, made it possible for my parents to buy this place. When my father fretted and stalled she said, "I'm buying it," and buy it she did. It cost her twelve hundred dollars. We stayed the next summer at Mrs. Zwicker's—taking meals home-style in the dining room with one other family and a sprinkling of bird-watchers and watercolorists. We spent two weeks plastering, patching, and painting a house too shambled to live in. None of the work was hired out. My father's parsimony was a Yankee trait. For him hardship and integrity were cut from one cloth.

RAIN. ITS CRYSTAL DARTS FLICKERING DOWN, TAPPING ON THE quiet; its sheen lighting up the woods. Rain keeps me inside, changes my plans from the daylong hike, the joy of solitude in the woods, back into the needful house where I barely keep up with the peeling, leaking collapse of the place.

"MABOU'S EXTREMITY MAKES IT A STATION WHERE NATURE'S intensities shape the life of the spirit," W. S. Di Piero writes on Robert Frank's Mabou, Nova Scotia.

AN ASTROLOGER ONCE TOLD ME THAT MY PAST WAS A BAG FULL of groceries that had ripped and spilled all over the planet. It was my task in this life to pick up the groceries. If I felt drawn to a place, if the longing persisted for more than a day, I should go there. Mostly I come to Castalia and let the place happen to me.

ONE DROUGHT-BURNED SUMMER A NEIGHBOR, GIVING ME directions to a public spring piped out of the woods, told me that *Castalia* was an Indian word meaning *beautiful spring*. Another said the name was biblical. Pick any tradition, just make it ancient, seemed to be the rule of thumb. The encyclopedia says Castalia was a spring on Mount Parnassus, sacred to Apollo and the Muses, and regarded as the source of inspiration. Our Castalia was most likely named by a well-schooled reactionary, a Loyalist to the British Crown, as were most of the island's early settlers, bolting from the terrifying radicalism of the American Revolution. Castalia isn't much of a town. It's a stretch of road, a leg of woods, a steep bank dropping to a stony beach, a postal code, convenience store, cluster of houses—a place that makes me stretch into unplanned labors and unplotted thoughts.

I WASHED OUT CLOTHES IN THE SINK TODAY, DESPITE THE FOG, hanging them on a wooden rack beside the kitchen stove. By afternoon the weather had broken and I hauled the stuff outside. I thought it might offend the more religious islanders that I hung out my brightly colored underwear on Sunday—a double offense that I had labored on the Lord's day and that turquoise and purple might suggest I took pleasure in my body. I remembered a film about laundry, which a folklorist friend had shown—women interviewed about their laundry experiences and their telling of methodologies, family dynamics, the joy of hanging all the similar colors in a group, each woman's unique ritual. My friend then spoke about how art exists on a continuum ranging from the backyard to the Louvre, how artmaking gives meaning to daily life—intention and resonance. She asked the audience to recall their own laundry stories, which spanned from washboard in a wilderness stream to grungy laundromat. I remembered doing wash by hand with my mother in the backyard of the Connecticut house where I grew up, wringing the wet clothes into coiled snakes of cloth, then hanging them out to dry. The clothesline ran along the curving edge of a small lawn that dropped steeply down into woods. I remembered the space created when sheets were hung along the line, forming a kind of outdoor room with billowing white walls.

My second laundry memory was of a house in Maine where I had lived for several years. Out the backdoor a clothesline ran on a pulley into an enormous maple tree. That pulley had seemed a luxury to me after living through years of poverty and struggle as a single mother. What could it have cost—a six-inch-diameter gizmo available in any hardware store? But luxury for me had less to do with expense and more to do with pleasure. What joy to wheel our fragrant clothing out into the dappled maple sun, to worship ordinary sunlight—the god of ritual and transformation that inspired me to hang out the wash and be purified.

I'VE NEVER UNDERSTOOD THE RABID EMOTIONS WITH WHICH people separate evolution from God, God from the body. Why do the devout need suddenness—human life as the brand new product on the shelf produced *deus ex machina*—as proof of the Divine? Darwin, troubled by dreams of being beheaded or hanged, realized that stating his belief in evolutionary process was "like confessing a murder." But evolution is godly, its bias toward enhancing collective survival at the price of individual life, the origin of morality. Each body is a storehouse of godly decisions made in the complex biological improvisation of Earth, nature the divine chronographer, genetic chance (the DNA as dice) is God—the inventor, the intelligence, the luck behind us all.

I SCRAPE AND PAINT THE PORCH. A KNEE-BLISTERING, MISERABLE job that needs doing every two or three years in this saturated climate. Once I nearly broke my ankle stepping through a rotten slat. Since then I mark the punky wood with stones until I get around to mending it. Always plenty of scrap lumber washed up on the beach. I have inherited from my father the pleasure of fixing up while making do.

My neighbor Lester stops by while I'm hard at it, laughs and says, as if he's giving testimony to a celestial jury, "Yes, she did a lot of work on her knees. She had the right position, but I don't know if she had the right words."

WAITING IN LINE AT THE FERRY TERMINAL TO BUY A TICKET I OVER-hear two old-timers.

"Poor old Gleason—didn't get to see the new ferry."

"Just goes to show you how fast a person can get out of here."

Heads shaking back and forth.

"They say the swallow population's dying off."

"Aren't enough flies this year."

ON THE DAY HE DIED GLEASON HAD STOPPED BY. I WAS SITTING on the porch rubbing ice on the bee stings I'd suffered clipping out brush on the trail down to the beach. We sat in the old Adirondack chairs and jawed at trivial injustices. He turned on that good-hearted smile that everyone loved him for. The man could still flirt with charm in his nineties.

"If I was just a few years younger," he'd said, "I'd go down there with a scythe and find that bee's nest for you. Used to be a lot of bees on this island—on every blossom of clover."

That night he'd been sitting in his kitchen, felt a little funny, called up his daughter and by the time she swung into his driveway he was gone.

THE WRINKLERS HAVE STOPPED AGAIN TODAY, PARKING THEIR pickup in front of the cottage to walk down to the stone beach. They carry burlap sacks and five-gallon plastic buckets—a middle-aged woman and two teenage sons. Ours is the only decent trail cutting down the forty-foot drop along the Castalia Bank.

Wrinklers pick periwinkles off the rocks at lowtide. It's slithery, tedious, barnacle-cutting-the-fingertips work. But a fast wrinkler can make good pay, and some islanders earn a modest living harvesting wrinkles and the other readymade cash crop—dulse. Periwinkles are sea snails about the size of a thimble. Steamed in wine, garlic, and basil they make a delicate pasta sauce guaranteed to leave one hungry. I don't know where they are sold or what they are used for commercially, only that after several hours the wrinklers climb back up the bank carrying lumpy sacks full.

The trail down the bank is my pride, and I'm glad to know that it's used year-round by islanders. It used to be a rutted woodchuck path that sneaked under a backbreakingly low apple bough, through a patch of stinging nettles, down a gravel-skidding incline to the beach. Going down was a calamity and climbing up was a trial. There were echoes of a more utilitarian trail in the evenly paced footfalls buried like the foundation of an ancient city beneath the weedgrass. Over the span of several summers I trimmed back the overgrowth, cleared boulders, set and braced posts for a railing. Scrap lumber tends to float over from the harbor to our beach, so there is an annual crop for me to pick through—birch and cedar poles left over from the topping off of weir stakes. If I walk a mile down the beach I'm sure to find posts, rails, and bracing stakes that fit exactly to the job's specifications. Failing that, I change the project's design so that the posts and rails rarely need a cut. I enjoy matching the need to the find—doing so with the eye, not measuring anything. The point and the pleasure has been to build and repair the railing without buying anything except nails. My father lived this pleasure to a fault, so set on making do that when he died he left us with two houses listing from wear and a collection of unusable tools—divot in the screwdriver blade, broken-handled hammer, coffee can of rusted square-cut salvaged nails, a scythe dull as stone, and a hatchet from the Pleistocene. I have made some concessions to technology in buying a steel-shank hammer, a bow saw, and an ax with a fiberglass handle. I add one or two tools to the collection each year and they glitter in the shed like a newly discovered constellation.

This year I have only one post to repair on the railing—the top one, which takes the most stress—a steep leg up the last rise from the bank to the lupine meadow. I dismantle the last section of railing and unearth the teetering post. It has taken me ten years to learn how to set a fence post that will stay straight for more than a season. Ten years of trial and error, how-to pamphlets, and observation in the field. I widen the hole with a stake, place the new post—lucky to have found one already sharpened to a crude point—pound it as far into the ground as it will go, then replace the soil, tamping it frequently to keep the fit snug. I set a shorter bracing post four feet away, out of line with the rail posts, and nail a diagonal between the two to create some stabilizing triangulation. Finally I nail on the railing—a fresh birch pole still holding its bark, pleasingly smooth to the touch, sturdy and green enough to vibrate but not lean under the weight of a wrinkle-bearing climber.

Swallowtail Light. Best place onshore to watch whales. Family with videocam picnicking. Finbacks and porpoises feeding offshore, arcing and diving—sleek, silent, black. "Awesome," cries the man from Toronto. "What's that I'm seeing?" He's suddenly younger than his little son, who's just confused. "Did you see it, Warren?" Dad keeps hollering, the whales feeding languidly, raising flukes to make a deep dive.

"We were hoping to see a right whale," he tells me, suddenly disappointed when I explain that these three are finbacks.

Everyone longs to see the last-gasp species—the whale our ancestors hunted most voraciously to the brink because it was the "right" whale to kill for its bounty of oil. Now it's the right whale for sighting. We love that these lost ones are coming back, their numbers increasing each year. They give us hope for ourselves—

the strange race our species seems to run between our intelligence and our rapacious stupidity.

OVERHEARD AT THE HARDWARE STORE:
"That orange cat of yours has a pretty yellow bird in its mouth."
"Anhh, don't worry about it. That's just its human nature."

I WORK OVER MY NOTES FROM THE ISLAND WHILE SITTING IN A park in Flagstaff, Arizona. Laptop parked on a picnic table. Ponderosa pines all around. Two squirrels cavort through the clearing—a romp or a fight—I can't tell which. Then I look up to see through the matrix of tree trunks a large shining black animal loping toward me. Bear? elk? feral dog? I rapidly sort mental files, blood revved to red alert. It's a huge Doberman, tense enough to lunge, and the startle reflex jolts me up from the table, sorting this time how to protect myself—under the table? on the run? Just as I reach for my keys—as if they'll do me any good—the owner jogs into view, calls back the dog, and leashes it.

Of all the roles animals play in my life, this animal tension—the moment of panic and the moment of relief—is most stirring. To be an animal is to know this sensation of wildness, electric as sexual arousal. Sometimes I think our species dominates others in an attempt to be free of such bodily alarms—the jolt of chemical energy that warns of a violent death. Yet where other than in our own bodies could we hope to know nature so well?

Women know this when they menstruate, the cycle reminding us monthly that we are controlled, at least in part, by biological forces not subject to will. Women know this who have given birth—an experience that surely should be ranked among any species' most heroic. By the eighth month of pregnancy, any woman with her eyes open knows that she has trekked into a fearsome wilderness from which there is no turning back. In labor she howls like a shot animal, lost to everything but pain, until she speaks her first words as a mother: "I want to protect you from everything."

HARLEY SHAW, WRITING ON THE RANGING BEHAVIOR OF ARIZONA mountain lions: "Home is the entire area of use."

HARDHACK. THE ISLANDERS' NAME FOR THIS WEED, THOUGH THE guidebook calls it steeplebush. *Spiraea tomentosa.* And a torment it is in the lupine meadow. One summer, intending to open more scrapland for walking, I made a sidecut trail off the grassy span we've managed to keep open across the road from our cottage. My father had cleared the meadow of alder and hardhack so that we'd have a water view from our porch. He carried wild lupine seed in his pockets from anywhere he could find it to make the place flower, marking the fragile spread palms of new lupines with tiny stakes to protect them from the swing of his blade. I've tried to keep the meadow up since he died, counting the blossoms every year as a hedge against the loss of his passing. Of course, wildflowers don't really work to stave off grief. But the spires of violet, fuschia, and blue bring his presence to mind. And when I work among the lupines, whether in flower or rattling their hairy dried pods, I feel that I work by his side.

Opening the sidecut using dull clippers to make a pass through the thicket of bestial hardhack was mean work. Hardhack grows in thigh-deep clusters, the woody stalks forming an intricate undergrowth that is all but invisible beneath a layer of woolly leaves and fuzzy pink pyramids of tiny flowers, blooms not unlike those of the domestic shrub spiraea. No tool that I own works against this weed. Too densely clustered for scythe, sickle, or long-bladed clippers. Too coarse for the neighbor's weedwhacker. Too abundant for pruning shears—like plowing snow with a teaspoon. The only hope of clearing such land is to start on the perimeter, where one can get a purchase on the excrescence, and to remind oneself frequently of the virtue of patience.

I enjoyed the sidecut for that one summer, walking through shoulder-high blackberries, feet scrunching over the stubble of hardhack, then dead-ending at a fallow old apple tree, turning around and heading out. Only a ten-minute walk—but ground I was happy to cover. William James said that those things most ours are those we've claimed by work. I called that scrappy little passage mine. The next summer, intent upon extending my domain by another ten minutes, I hastened with newly sharpened clippers back to the site. The hardhack had reclaimed every inch.

TWO

 # INSIDE THE WOLF

It is so dark inside the wolf.
—The Brothers Grimm

IN THE COMMUNITY ROOM EIGHT PATIENTS GATHERED
for meals. Helen, a coarse gray boulder of a woman with her head
half-shaved, tapped her tray and sang "La-ba-ba-ba-ba-bamba,"
laughing and shuffling a joke of a foot dance in her wheelchair
when the therapist asked her to lift her leg. Gladys, a curled stump,
asked everyone else's visitor, "Will you get me a drink of water?
Will you tell them I have to go?" The patients wore sweatsuits,
each person strapped for safety into a wheelchair modified to suit
the damage the nervous system had suffered—this one's doll-like
left arm velcroed to an armrest, another trussed to a booster to prevent her from slipping out of the chair onto the floor. One day two
new men were brought in. The first with a glazed expression—no
affect at all to the face. He was greeted by a nervously cheerful
young man. "Hello, I'm a doctor. I will be your general internist.
I will work with you here in rehab, and I want you to know I won't
do anything you don't want me to do." The glazed man, just as
businesslike, replied, "Hello. I'm a patient." The other new man
was a tall patrician type and not visibly impaired. He looked just
a bit tired and remote. Later it appeared that he no longer could
speak. His wife came in with the flurried energy of the outside,
swirling fashionably, a woman who seemed to have been denied no
comforts. She kissed the top of his head and said with pride, "Well,
you've had a very good report!" The rest of us, visiting our damaged loved ones, looked at each other and thought, she's got a lot
to learn. How the brain swells after a stroke. How the real dam-

age takes weeks to assess. How we cut the food, place the dishes on the unimpaired side. How we encourage, we cheer, we resist feeding them so they will learn to scoop the Jell-O to their lips for themselves. How one family watches another's patience. How we turn away and weep at another family's love.

We were not prepared for my father's heart attack coming on Christmas Eve of his eighty-third year just days after playing his weekly tennis match, hauling downed limbs out of the woods for firewood, cutting a Norway spruce he'd grown himself and dragging it to the house for the holiday festivities. Old age had not stopped him from being a physical man, taking such pleasure in working in the woods and yard that I often thought he should have been a forester or an organic farmer, rather than a radio announcer and public relations man. The family prides itself on longevity and Ben (my brother and I always called our father by his name) was the most vigorous and even-tempered of five siblings all of whom were thriving in their seventies and eighties. The good death in our family was my great-uncle Fred's; he died tipping back his third martini in celebration of a rousing tennis match at Forest Hills. If death must come, our family legend would say, let it be swift, let it find me in action, let it not weaken my work or my joy. It was not only vigor and genes that kept my father's generation young, but their stubborn refusal of weakness, their New England faith in the power of persistence itself—a faith inspired by the rugged hills of our Connecticut home ground, which could surface an annual crop of stones more readily than one of turnips. We were even less prepared for the stroke, which came three months after he had fought his way back from the heart attack.

"What are those bugs all over the walls?" he asked me from his hospital bed.

"I don't know."

"They're Egyptian carpet crickets. They came on cargo ships and they're devastating the oriental carpet business in this country and in the world." His voice grew earnest, the radio journalist in him speaking.

"There aren't any in the hospital," I tried to reassure.

"Yes, there are. They come in here with the people. I've seen them as big as lobsters. An Egyptian carpet merchant told me what they were."

His manner was lucid. Though signals were misfiring, there was a characteristic charm to his hallucinations. My father always was a charming man—the kind who warmed a room with his presence.

"The Lord is the best dentist," he told his sister when she came to the hospital to visit. This from a man who had not been to church since 1920, when as a teenager he was taken by his aunt Adelaide to communion at the Litchfield Congregational Church and, finding the ritual cannibalistic, refused to go back.

"Why?" replied his sister.

"Because He does the most with teeth."

The most telling delusion he suffered had to do with his realizing something he had always wanted. When I visited him on the day after the stroke, he believed that he had won a literary contest sponsored by the *Hartford Courant*, that an award check for $350 had come in the mail the day before. He clearly remembered the note from the editor saying, "This is certainly explicit." He remembered that the award was for a story that dealt with extreme emotional loss and that he had won with "Goodbye, Adela"—an actual story of his about the death of his tyrannical aunt Adelaide. The bad news was that the check had been hanging from his bed in a plastic bag and was left in the ultrasound lab. All that was hanging there now was a sack of his urine. So convincing was his account of this misfortune, that he had succeeded in sending nurses and orderlies to track down his winnings. He bristled when I questioned whether it had happened.

"I know what happened," he insisted, outraged that I should question his judgment.

The neurologist told him there was no award, the incident never had happened, and advised us to help bring him back to the facts. But it was difficult to know what was best for him—to correct his error of perception or to let him have the pleasure that his need for literary recognition had found a reward. The fantasy seemed a small consolation to grant him for losing a part of his brain.

What was most disconcerting was that he sounded entirely coherent even when his brain scrambled signals. One evening when I was about to leave the hospital he urged me to drive carefully and to listen to the weather on the radio.

"Conditions can change fast along the coast," he cautioned.

"I don't have to drive up the coast tonight, Ben. I'm just going home to Mom."

"No," he said, "you are home."

"No, I'm not," I said. "Do you know where you are?"

"Of course I do," he fumed, "I'm on the tenth floor of the Danbury Hospital, Room 29."

"Right," I said. "So, I'm going home now."

"But you are home."

"Well, I'll see you in the morning."

Not only was his left side paralyzed, but his perception of leftness was shot, a disruption of spatial perception common after damage to the right parietal lobe. When he reached with his right hand to grasp the left hand, he reached all the way down to his knee, as if he believed the arm to fill that much space. He worked at building the movement back into his leg and fingers. He learned to drive a wheelchair, but kept wheeling into the wall, smashing a finger, which had to be dressed with a bandage and salve, or colliding with another patient's wheelchair. He had a cracked rib, which he claimed was caused when an orderly came to change his sheets, flipped him into the air and spun him around three times, slamming him down against the bedrail.

"Watch your left," we reminded him.

"That's right," he said attentively, wheeling into the wall or

someone's ankle. The doctor told him that the stroke had left him
with a spatial problem he would have to work on. Think left, think
left, all the time. But how could he know what no longer existed
for him? How could he think it? It must have been like trying to
access a sense he never had. He worked diligently at rehabilitation
exercises, but he did not seem to mourn the loss of anything. His
dumb left hand would lie in the middle of his dinner and he would
look at it with idle curiosity. He no longer owned it, the hand that
had earned him humiliation at school—"Benton suffers from left-
handedness that cannot be corrected"—the hand that had deftly
tied fishing flies, pulled ribbons of news from the teletype machine,
written stories and plays, wielded cigarettes and microphones and
ski poles, the hand that had caressed and aroused my mother
before I was born.

"My legs feel like stalks of overcooked asparagus," my father
cracked when the occupational therapist tried to get him to slip on
his sweats. Two weeks after the stroke he had regained some movement in the left arm and leg, but he still could not push his arm
through a sleeve. "Oh, yes," he answered the therapist, then immediately forgot, his eyes drifting back to the television elbowing off
the wall. It took two health workers to help him take a shit, to
move him from bed to wheelchair, from wheelchair to toilet, to
reassure him that the seat was underneath him while he battled
with spatial distortion on the way down to the seat. Two workers
to balance and wipe him, to pull up his pants, and heave him back
into his chair. His days were structured with occupational and
physical therapy sessions. He worked on identifying shapes, copying words, fitting pegs in holes; on leg lifts and assisted walking—
through awkward repetition of tasks attempting to restructure the
neural networks. His speech had not been affected by the stroke,
which blossomed on the right side of his brain, so other than base-
line testing, the speech therapist had left him alone. He took comfort in the structure of the daily schedule. He was a serious student
of his own recovery. On weekends, when fewer staff were on duty,

group sessions met in the community room—eight chairs in a circle, a foam beach ball tossed around to the tune of a crackling
record. "Let's re-mem-ber Pearl Har-bor and go on to vic-to-ry...."

There was the social worker who called my mother in for a con-
sultation.

"Have you considered what you will do if your husband does
not recover? Have you thought about a nursing home?"

"My husband will never go to a nursing home."

"On two days' notice he could be sent to another unit ..." She
explained Medicare regulations, how many days remained before
the coverage would run out, the government's discharge require-
ments established to contain the cost of health care. My mother
heard none of it, convinced that he would recover, come home, and
thrive under her care.

There was the "family orientation meeting" with the physician,
where we learned the modest discharge goals after a proposed
nine-week stay in the rehab unit—that he would be capable of
"assisted mobility." We tried to learn the language—"acute" conditions versus "chronic," "skilled" and "intermediate" and "custo-
dial care." Medicare, we learned, only pays if the patient is going
to get better. I made lists of questions, wanting a degree of clarity
impossible to attain given the circumstances. What role could we
as the family play in making decisions about his release? Would his
therapy continue if he went to the nursing home? What if we
couldn't afford nursing home care? What specific damage had
there been to the heart, to the brain? What degree of recovery
could we expect?

My mother went into emotional vertigo during these sessions.
The business of her husband's illness was a language she was incapable of mastering. During these conferences her attention would
spin out of the room and I would be left making promises to a
putty-faced social worker that I would take care of the necessary
paperwork for nursing homes, for state aid, for whatever purgato-
rial circle the health care system would send him to. When we

drove home from the hospital my mother would gird herself in a heroic posture.

"This is my time to be great," she said, believing, I suppose, that her commitment would be sufficient for the demands of his care. There was no room to consider that she might have to help him to die, or that we might drift from one vague week to the next, uncertain whether to hope for his recovery or his death. As a family we lacked the ability to bridge the gap between the seriousness of his condition and our vision of what loving entailed.

During his last hellish eighteen months, when he endured a heart attack, two strokes, Legionnaires' disease, and pneumonia, he became surprisingly adaptable. Each time he returned home from the hospital he came back further diminished—remote, dazed by the confusion taking over his body. There was no comfort we could give him for this. None he could give us. His vigorous life had slowed to an idle. He remained disgusted with politics, oil spills, and big money. He sat at the card table reading every page of junk mail, sending off for giveaways and sweepstakes, fulfilling the silly rules—stickers and checkoffs, peel-off Jaguars and mansions. Who could fault him? He still felt that the world owed him something. He remained generally hopeful, even willing to joke about his condition.

"What a big boy! I took three steps today without falling down!"

With my mother the most tender moments were often the most painful. The times I treasure are not when she would insist, "He will get better, he has to get better, that's all that we can say." Rather they are the times when the measure of her grief gave dimension to her love, as one night when we came home from the hospital to her hollow living room, and she wept, saying, "That beautiful man is gone … our beautiful time together, gone." And later, "Unavoidable, what you think can't happen to you. In the end you're alone."

Once she dreamed she was in a field—a Fellini movie she called it. Her friend Betty Wick, who had lost her husband three years previously, was making pita breads. Mom was spreading them with butter and eating them. "I kept worrying I'd get fat, but I kept eating them." Death was the cloying meal she feared, the meal she couldn't refuse.

I HAVE THOUGHT OF THE HOSPITAL AS A PLACE IN NATURE, A PECU-liarly desperate invention of our species born of our love of life and our passionate resistance to death. And I have begun to think of death, too, as a place in nature—"Yes," the Tohono O'ohdam elder said to my Yaqui friend, "it's a place in the desert right over there." Death is our home—where we all go at the end. I mean this quite literally—space and time being one—that the end of time each of us must experience is the one place we all share in common, and therefore a place we must not defile.

What makes our species unique is not our language, use of tools, consciousness, emotions, or morality. All these functions are manifest in other creatures, albeit in more rudimentary forms. What makes our species unique is our foreknowledge of death and the ritual with which we treat the dead. Skulls and limb bones arranged in ossuaries, ceremonial binding and positioning for burial, the funerary pyre, amulets and rice and honey placed in the tomb, pyramids and catacombs and mortuary sculpture, prayers and dances and keening for the dead, cleansing and dressing and cosmetically beautifying the dead, drinking and eating together in their memory. If, as Philippe Aries says, familiarity with death is a form of acceptance of the order of nature, then our contemporary distancing from death is a symptom of our disjunction with nature. Or perhaps the knowledge of death is the very malaise that causes the symptom of our being at odds with nature.

Aries also suggests that concepts of death are culturally constructed and what today we call the good death, the beautiful death is what used to be considered the accursed death. Gawain saw and knew death's approach—"Know ye well that I shall not live two days." Formerly one carried the knowledge of one's death within one, wrote Rilke, "as a fruit its kernel.... One *had* it, and that gave one a singular dignity and a quiet pride." Our contemporary sensibility is more akin to Montaigne's—"I want death to find me planting cabbages." May death come, we plead, without warning, without my suffering—may it take me unaware. Death and dying, once made tame by nearness, by their presence in our homes, are now relegated to the terrifying wilderness of hospitals. The work of the hospital is to prevent death, not to facilitate deathbed reconciliations or to witness death's approach as an expression of faith in destiny or in the completeness of nature.

I have lived for forty-six years and I have never touched a corpse, have seen only one—the body of my grandfather plastered into a coffin up to which I could barely reach my six-year-old gaze. He was just a suit in a box past which I filed. My first death terrors came when I was twelve and my great-uncle Henry Hawthorne died. He had been a cranky eccentric, but I had loved his playful belligerence. "Who are *you?*" he'd scowl at me at breakfast when I visited the family homestead. "Alison," I'd say, and he'd fume back, "I didn't know Al had a son." I remember overhearing the grown-ups conducting the business of his death—the wording of the obituary and whether or not his ashes would arrive in time for the burial service. The inconceivable hit me like a high-speed train. He was nothing now, forever. I would be too. All the longed for, strived for, hard-won sense of who I might become would amount to a cupful of ash. Nothing seemed crueler than the idea of my own inevitable death. It kept me awake with the light on for weeks, poisoned every pleasure and ambition, became the bitter torque of a hostile universe that made anything beautiful—a zucchini blossom, a bluebird, or an opera—a rotten joke.

There were few death rituals, no ministers or priests, little visible grief in my family. People just disappeared and became the stories others remembered of them. Those who remained improvised

an ending for the departed ones that seemed to suit their character—my great-aunt Gwen was scattered in the woods she loved,
while Henry was planted under a simple black stone in the family
plot. Sometimes those who gathered at the graveside were so sad-
dened that no one could say a word. They simply wept stiffly
around the absence. As deaths have accumulated I have begun to
think of life and death as a set of balance scales. When one is
young, the scale is heavily tipped toward the living. With the first
death, the first consciousness of death, the counter scale begins to
fall. Death by death, the scales shift weight until what was unthinkable becomes merely a matter of gravity and the fall into death
becomes an easy step.

I have helped one cancer-ridden friend to die, if helping means
to look unflinchingly with him at that prospect while trying to
bring to his bedside after brain surgery what of life he continued
to crave—in this case, miso soup, yellowtail sashimi, good company, and no pity. I homesteaded as a part-time farmer in northern Vermont for ten years, serving as midwife and butcher to
lambs, pigs, rabbits, chickens, and turkeys. I wanted to understand
what it meant to be a carnivore, wanted my daughter to know
cycles of living and dying. A farmer would not be deceived by the
tidy wrapped packages at the supermarket as to the dependence in
nature of one living thing upon the life of another. Still, I admit
that I don't know much about death and the sorriest lesson I've
learned is that words, my most trusted guardians against chaos,
offer small comfort in the face of anyone's dying. One has finally
a paltry vocabulary to offer—to hold the hand, to stroke the hair
back from the face, to say again "I love you"—words we hope will
be the final anchor line tossed ashore. Too often when the dying
set sail, the living are left with the toxic spill of their suffering to
clean up.

ON EASTER THE REHAB STAFF WORE BUNNY EARS, TAILS, AND puffy slippers. There was a flower on each tray, yellow-and-purple paper napkins, a basket with a chocolate bunny, and jelly beans for each patient. Paper rabbits and colored eggs were taped up to the walls. After two months living in the rehab unit, my father's mobility had improved just enough for him to be a danger to himself. The staff began strapping him to his chair to keep him from falling. He became impatient, couldn't stand the hospital another ten days until his scheduled release. He called Mom on the telephone every night at bedtime like a homesick kid away at camp.

"Sometimes," he said, "I just want to run as fast as I can down the corridor." He could sit and walk with cues—a litany of self-instruction required to keep his movements coordinated—"Cane, left, right. Cane, left, right." Often the words bore no relation to his actions, but he voiced them diligently and was befuddled when he would stumble into the therapist's arms. I dreamed he walked freely, Mom and I strolling on ahead of him in our woods, looking back anxiously to find that he could simply walk—didn't forget his left side, didn't crumple or tangle his drooping foot, didn't walk into a tree or a gully. When I woke, it seemed that that accomplishment would erase every disappointment and heartache in him and that was all I wanted for him, that he might just walk with us again. Then came the bad news that his stay had been extended another month. It was good news to us in that we knew we would be unable to care for him at home in his damaged condition. But for him the prolonged stay was further punishment. While we, at home in our grief, could stare out the living room window into the winter pond, where golden carp had burrowed for protection under the silt, where torn willow leaves lay scattered on the shallows and the moon sprawled its oystery light across the black water, he was left to the long hospital nights broken with measurements and medicine, the loneliness of fellow patients after their visitors had gone, the contagious corridors echoing with the terror of the dying and the terror of those being born.

He was scolded by the nurse when he stood up by his bedside to dial home. She stormed into the room.

"You're not supposed to do that alone. You didn't call me ...," though by then ringing his buzzer for assistance had become a joke. He was no priority on a floor where the new admissions couldn't swallow without assistance, where one woman had a grid of steel pins protruding from the meat of her calf and thigh, where another screamed at one-thirty every morning as if she were being murdered.

"And no one knows why she does it," my father reported more curious than troubled. He hated the scoldings and stood up again to call home and complain.

The first time I saw my father treated like a child because he was old occurred several years earlier when he was still in good health. We had gone out to eat at a Chinese restaurant and he had ordered wine. There was some minor confusion about which wine he wanted, an awkwardness on his part when the waitress questioned him. Though he was socially gracious, my father's thriftiness had meant he never bothered to become an oenophile. Jug wine would do at home, and he ate in restaurants so rarely that the sophisticated rituals of wine selection required him to play a role in which he was ill-rehearsed. At his hesitation the waitress suddenly leaned close, shifted her tone to one of condescension as if she were addressing a troublesome, slow-witted child who had tried her patience too long. A dimension of his character was erased with her voice, and he became simply an old man. I suppose that this social erasure, which is common treatment toward older people in our culture, is an expression of denial. No one wants to acknowledge that the shriveling of the face, the distorting compression of the spine, the thickening of joints, and the slowing of mental actions are inevitable for anyone lucky enough to have a long life. Easier to dismiss those thus afflicted as "the old" without trying to picture their seamless faces at sixteen, their once muscular verve, their eagerness at half a dozen junctures for the next chapter of life, their still unfolding stories—complicated, quirky, theirs alone.

My father never saw himself as an old man. I don't believe he ever thought that he would die. Or if he thought it, he shared the terrors with no one. The closest he came was to quip, "Isn't it fun coming here to watch your father disintegrate?" Even my mother, his devoted mate for fifty-five years, wrote to me after his death, "I only wish I had known some of the deeper parts of him that always remained buried within."

I pictured him looking me right in the eye and saying, "I'm going to die." And my reply, "Yes, are you afraid?" But such directness was never possible. I dreamed that I was bathing him, that I left the room so he could relax in the tub a while and returned to find him unconscious, submerged. This happened repeatedly. I would lift his frail white body by the waist and he would slump forward from my arms. I would lean close to see if he was breathing— yes, I think so. I dreamed he came home attached to a gigantic machine—buttons, dials, and graphs—the size of a carnival trailer. Sallow, gaunt, and dull, he closed his eyes when the machine shut off, opened them when the motor hummed. I thought of the brain and the mind, how a mechanism so complicated and refined—a result of a million accidents of natural selection—made it possible for me to grieve and to write my grief down. I thought of the brain's materiality—one hundred billion neurons and their ability to instantly integrate thousands of functions—and its transcendence of the material in harboring a resonant inner life. And I hoped my father's brain was sufficiently in control to produce endorphins or some such inborn sedative to ease him away from witnessing his own dissolution.

HIS RETURN STAY AT HOME LASTED ALMOST A YEAR—A YEAR OF junk mail, teetering on his cane, visiting nurses and therapists, frailty and diligent exercising, slow gains and the comfort of being in his own place. I shuttled back and forth from my apartment and job in Provincetown, providing inadequate respite for my mother whose full-time job had become his care. I shoveled through the Augean stables of his medical bills and health insurance forms, covered the tulip beds with chicken wire so the deer wouldn't nip off the new buds, and occasionally knew the satisfaction of finding the right words to light the inarticulate darkness through which one or another of us foundered.

But kindness in word or deed generally fell short of the need that occasioned them. He longed for the woods, which had always been his place of meditation, his escape from the necessary trivialities of domestic existence. One day at his cajoling I walked with him on my arm up a slight incline into the laurel and hickory scrub past the barn. We made it only a few dozen yards before he became breathless and frightened. He must have wondered then, though neither of us spoke it, at what point does one give up on life because limitation makes it no longer worth living. That evening my mother and I listened cautiously to the heave of his sleeping breath, the danger in his snore. He woke to chest pains. We placed nitro under his tongue to kick his heart back up to speed. My mother began to spin away. I pulled a chair to the bedside and made her sit. She held his hand and stroked his precious arm for a beautiful half hour. Please take him here and now, I prayed to death. He puzzled tensely, trying to deflect the symptoms. "I don't have angina. There was no damage to the heart muscle." Though he ran through the repertoire of reassurances, we all felt death's presence in the bedroom. Then he went to sleep. In the morning, fine and up for breakfast, he admitted that he'd thought it was "the big one." We fell to explaining why he'd had the close call—the walk was too much for him, the outpatient rehab program too strenuous—as if death's nearness indicated some failure of our collective will or wisdom, rather than a message from the inevitable.

During that period at home, when he was struggling to relearn how to walk and to write his name, I found a letter hacked out in his typewriter. Months after my mother and I had forgotten the delusion of his literary award, had thought it had passed for him as well, we realized how alone he was inside his damaged brain, how impossible it was for him to believe what we had told him.

> July 11, 1989
> Editor, Northest Magazine.
> dear Larry Bloom:
> this is a paculiar letter, I mutst address toyo. It concerns a short story I submitted to your magazine titled "goodby Adela. I sent it to you last January the precise date evades me. However on March 6th I suffered a major cerebral stroke that left my left side totally paralyzed and my right side seriously imparied. On March 7th I belive I received in the mail a letter form the H.C. enclosing a check for $335 as payment for First Prize in the Courants SS Contest.
> In the turmoil and confusion of getting admitted to the Danbury Hospital the letter and check got lost. I changed beds three times the first morning and the letter and its contents as far as I can figure got lost in the bedding.
> When I related the entire episode to my neurollogist, he said, "Forget it Ben. It never happened. I assured him it had, and he explained. Ben you're hallucinating. you never received such a letter. your injured brain made it up to recompense you for your injury by rewarding you with somthing that had very deep meaning to you. Forget it, It never happened.
> So clear and "real" is my recollection of the letter, the color, the type, and the comment of yours on the story that I was compelled to write, with the hope that you can clarify the issue—FACT, or hallucination.
> P.S. Due to the marvelous care at the H pdpitl's Rehabilitation c m er, I am not about 0% returned to normal.

THE FOLLOWING APRIL HE WAS READMITTED TO THE HOSPITAL, this time with pneumonia. I watched him decline over the course of an afternoon in an understaffed hospital ward. He rang the buzzer, moaning, "Nurse, please help me," then telling me, "No, I'm not in pain anywhere. That's just the way this buzzer system works. You ring again and again—forty-five minutes later they come."

"Try to sleep," I said.

"That's not as easy as it sounds," he replied.

"I know—just try to close your eyes."

"Maybe I can drop off."

Long quiet, then, "Life isn't always what it seems."

"Yes, I know," I answered, trying to calm him. In retrospect I wish I had asked what he meant—what could he see from that bleak vantage which I could not?

"I'm sorry," he said.

"For what?"

"This mess."

"You don't have to be sorry, just get better."

Quiet, eyes closed, the man in the next bed hacking, then, "This is very disagreeable."

During the afternoon he became more and more lost—unable to sit up in bed, dazed, vomiting, awareness drifting off, eyes scared wide, losing me and the room, then his left hand shaking against his belly, breathing hard as if he were about to come. I tried to bring the nurses to assess his decline, but whatever else was happening on the ward had taken precedence. He tried to piss. Couldn't. Held his drinking cup to his penis, his urine bottle to his lips, tried to put his false teeth in upside down. I became useless to him and I imagined throwing away all the bottles of pills, pulling out the IV tubes and nasal cannula, and bringing him home to die.

By the next morning he'd been moved to Intensive Care—the euphemism meant to soften the blow that all the patient gets is technology. The team of doctors huddled, patching together his history, the symptoms and signs. Was it pneumonia or heart failure? The agent—pneumococcus, mycoplasma, legionella? A tube pumped pure oxygen into his lungs, but his blood wasn't picking it up. His lungs filled with fluid. Unconscious. The intern asked me to leave the room while he pushed a rubber tube down my father's throat. Rusty fluids vacuumed from his gut and lungs. Dextrose, erythromycin dripping into his arm. A patch of nitro taped to the chest. By evening he was alert, though still intubated, a technician monitoring oxygen levels with a clip attached to finger or toe. I tried to tell him he was doing better, he wouldn't be on the machines for long. He grabbed my finger the way a baby does, a tear in the corner of each eye. He tried to speak, but his lips barely moved around the tube that inflated and deflated his chest like a dummy's. His words were just noise scraping up his throat.

Night. Morphine. Heparin injected directly through the belly muscle. The usual heart meds poured down the red tube. Then a can of Ensure. The IV for antibiotics. The ventilator's oxygen set at ninety-eight percent saturation. The hope was that enough will remained in his body to enable him to overcome the pneumonia that we now knew had been caused by legionella. A woman on the unit had been unconscious and on the ventilator for three months. And there were worse stories told in the waiting room of that unit. I learned to couch my excitement that my father was improving in deference to those for whom after months there was no change.

At some point while under the machines with Legionnaires' disease, he had another stroke. He came to and could breathe on his own, but his left side again had gone remote. He recovered sufficiently to move back down the hall into rehab, where he again recovered sufficiently to move back home. The last neurological effect of his brain damage was that he lost control of his emotions. Some bridge meant to keep one from being constantly overwhelmed with feeling had been washed out. At the smallest prompting—when I showed him a photo of a reworked traffic sign reading YIELD TO WHIM—he burst into this new weeping-laughing emotion, tears of joy and fullness spilling down his cheeks. The rehab staff told us that we should teach him to control these outbursts. Yet to see this gentle man moved by some holy spirit of emotional abundance was to be unable to deny him. This disability seemed to open him to the nourishment he required. Weeping, he called the nurses "angels of God" because "they do God's work every day." He began watching an evangelist on his hospital TV and reported soberly, a controlled tremble in his voice, "He has some good things to say."

This time he had come home from the hospital in bad shape—frail, incontinent, confused. My mother became worn out with worry, the endless details of his care, and sleep deprivation from helping him to piss four, five, or six times a night—helping him to stand, taking his weight on her shoulders while sliding down his pajama pants, then inserting his penis into the plastic urine bottle. She began to bark at him, her voice sharp and critical. His references to angels increased. He didn't seem to be hurt by her frazzled impatience. Far from it.

"If someone flew down out of the clouds right now for me, I wouldn't even be tempted," he said, speaking of his gratitude for her attentions. He fell down frequently, but luckily didn't hurt himself. Every time he got up from his chair, anyone else in the house went on alert. One night while I was home he fell on the bedroom floor during the nocturnal ritual. My mother couldn't get him back on his feet and she woke me. Together we remembered the physical therapist's directions and coached him back to bed—roll him onto his right side, then to the knees, then elbows on the bed and up.

"Stay put when Mom tells you to," I warned him, "or she'll have to tie you like they did in the hospital."

It was hell then in that house. One tormented night my father told my mother, "I'm killing you, I know I'm killing you." My mother hid the bullets to his rifle and shotgun—"In case he gets too desperate." In my own growing sleeplessness, I listened to thudding sounds that punctuated the gentle spring rain outside their woods-encircled house. I imagined deer bumping into the siding as they fed on shrubs then began to eat their way into the house, or my father mad as Lear wandering the grounds. The only comfort was to see that the disability that made him suffer—that he worked so hard to overcome in the same determined way he had dug a ditch by hand in the winter to find a leaking pipe, or spaded up the vegetable garden by hand rather than spending a dime to rent a tiller—in the end, that disability allowed his great and essential love for the world's beauty to be expressed.

We talked one afternoon standing by the picture window overlooking the stone-lined pond, a graceful widening of a noisy forest stream that gave the house its pastoral music. I was scheduled to leave for a month in California, where I told him I planned to work on a long poem about nature and intelligence. He began to tremble with feeling then burst into tears.

"That's so wonderful," he said, barely getting his cracking voice out of his mouth, then composing himself to elaborate. "I've thought so much about it lately—looking out the window here and thinking how everything in nature is planned. In winter the leaves die, blow off and the wind packs them in around the roots and trunks to protect the trees from the cold. And the rain—how the trees drink it and make oxygen." His cheeks streaming.

SOME SAY A PERSON CAN CHOOSE THE MOMENT OF DEATH. ONE friend's mother, having exhausted the hospital's technological offerings, lay on the brink for two days until her son arrived to hold her hand. Health professionals report that this is common. As is the patient's staving off of death beyond all reasonable expectations until a loved one says, "If you need to leave us now, it's all right." These stories suggest that many people cannot make their departure without being released by their loved ones. One of my father's cousins, who died suddenly and in relatively good health, refused to go until he could report the fact to his wife. She had been downstairs fixing breakfast and called to him that it was time to get up. When he did not appear or reply, she went upstairs to find him lying in bed. "I'm dead," he told her and he died. In contrast, my father seemed to choose not to die. A kind man, a gentle man, he let death walk all over him for nearly two years and still he couldn't say, "Enough."

"I just hope he wasn't too afraid," my mother lamented. What had happened suggested it had been otherwise for him.

Two weeks after my flight west he was taken by ambulance for the fourth time to Danbury Hospital. Tuesday, June 4th. Again, pneumonia. My mother sounded manic and exhausted on the phone.

"You made the right decision," I told her, offering what consolation I could from three thousand miles away. "Shall I come home?"

"No, no. It's not serious. He'll be home in two weeks."

Two days later he died.

I HAVE READ ABOUT THE RITUALS EMPLOYED IN OTHER CULTURES to ensure that the dead rest in peace. David Meltzer in *Death* (San Francisco: North Point Press, 1984), a stunning anthology of cross-cultural texts, quotes Sebeok and Ingemann's *Studies in Cheremis:*

> Special preparations for death are made as a person is dying. In some places a moribund person is placed on a bed of straw because of the belief that, if a person dies on a feather bed, he must count the feathers in it in the next life, or, if he dies on a felt mat, he must count the hairs in the felt. Sometimes the dying person requests the clothing in which he will be buried. Each one present asks the dying person to forgive him for any wrong he may have committed. The dying person gives his blessings to his children. Forgiveness for any possible unknown offense is often asked even after the person has died.

And this quoted from Bullock and Whitney's *Folklore of Maryland*:

> A door or window is often opened just before a death to allow the soul free egress; otherwise, death will not "come easy," for the soul sees no way of getting into the open.
>
> It was a custom often to receive into one's own mouth the last breath of the dying.
>
> Some people cover the looking glasses in a room where a dead person lies.
>
> Sometimes all the water in the house is emptied from pitchers, buckets, and such.
>
> After a death in a house, clocks are stopped, mirrors covered, bells muffled.

ON THE DAY MY FATHER DIED, MY PLANE WAS STRUCK BY LIGHTning. I had taken off from San Francisco at midnight, sat out the dawn on a long layover at O'Hare, then climbed back into the sky through a turmoil of flashing clouds. The flight had been delayed to wait for the thunderstorms to pass, but they hadn't and we took off anyway. I had been very close to my father since hearing the news, playing over and over the details of a horrible death, as if repetition of the story would tame it. He'd been in pain. Mom stroking his stomach and calling the nurses, who said, "It's just the medication." He panicked, screaming, "Get me my cane. I want to go home." Then the professionals descending like locusts—he was to be moved to Intensive or Cardiac Care. "You might as well go out for a while while they move him," the nurse told my mother, as if this were business with which she need not be detained. And she left, almost didn't return after errands, shopping—exhausted, just beginning to catch up on sleep. She got back. "I'd like to see my husband." And the nurse said, "I'm sorry, sit down." After the news, the nurse said, "You can see him now." But my mother refused. "I want to remember him alive."

There are worse deaths, to be sure—rape and torture, childhood disease, random bullet, head-on crash, AIDS, suicide, war. My own death on the same day as my father's, simultaneous with three hundred other flaming souls, had our plane gone down rather than flown blithely on after the boom and shudder, the copilot's palliative words at ten thousand feet. No end to the innovations of dying we've introduced on the planet. What was haunting about this death was the ineptitude of everyone concerned, the small steps any one of us could have made to ease his crossing over, had we acknowledged that he was knee-deep already in the River Styx. I pictured his last moments as a panic of procedures, the gurney surrounded by strangers each doing a specialized job—pumping the chest, finding a bloodway, monitoring pressure, forcing in tubes— all in pointless counterpoint to his pain and flailing. I pictured his body lying alone in a cinderblock room, letting go of its warmth. I pictured his soul tangled in the web of technology trying to get loose—no one opening the window.

During the long afternoon and evening before my flight back east, I climbed into the hills of the coastal range, watched the Pacific curl toward shore, picked wild lupines and California poppies from the grassy sprawl. I thought I had never been in a place more beautiful, and I was happy in my grief to share that beauty with him. His presence was close, but of what was it composed? An inkling of his voice, his face, his love—but not these. "You can talk to him today—he's waiting for you—now, while the soul hovers near the body," said a friend who had learned what I had not. And it was true. I talked with him—not willfully but simply finding words that seemed to answer my father's continued questioning. I said the things that came to me in that vivid dislocation. Useless and essential things. Words to hold him close, words to help him want to go.

The fog began to pillow in over the hills, the coyotes to wail and bark, and the solitary mountain lion, which stalks that terrain though no one ever sees it, slid through the wind-rippled grasses in my mind's eye.

And then I flew, sitting behind the black-smudged funnel of a jet engine that powered me over the dim land below—every second exiting from itself, leaving nothing behind but dissipating fumes. What place is this over which the reluctant red-eyed traveler passes—leaving the past, leaving the present, leaving the future—rivers that have dried leaving desiccated veins to mark their passage?

EXILED IN AMERICA

IF ONLY IT WERE POSSIBLE TO SEE THE UNBROKEN NEW England forest through the eyes of my Puritan ancestors, to eat porridge and bear grease beside them in a dirt-floored hut, to know the fears that kept them awake at night. Certainly they feared the wilderness, its darkness, beasts, and savages. Perhaps they feared the freedom for which they had risked their lives would let loose a dangerous wildness that dwelled captive inside them. They saw their own nature as depraved, yet they were visionaries bent on the radical improvement of humankind. I have wanted to understand these "Zionists," not only because they are family, but also because the story they began—leaving their homeland, separating themselves from nature as they knew it to graft themselves to a new continent—is a story still in process. We, their descendants, after having trashed the land for three hundred and fifty years, can hardly claim to have treated it as a home. What is the meaning of ancestry? What is the meaning of *this* ancestry? When I try to know those distant strangers I feel a gnarl inside myself where the authoritarian and the libertine tangle like scrapping dogs.

My ancestry is distinguished—the first American Hathorne (my great-great-grandfather Nathaniel changed the spelling to "Hawthorne") came from England in the 1630s and became one of the Fathers of Massachusetts, helping to establish domestic order and a code of justice in the pioneer colony. That was ten generations ago. Since then we've been judges and magistrates, seamen and merchants, authors and statesmen, artists, journalists, educators, psychologists, a founder of a religious order for the care of the incurably ill, and dozens of decent people devoted to raising and educating their children in a manner that would honor their cultured ancestry. And yet, bloody roots feed this tree. My Puritan ancestors committed brutal, shameful deeds in the name of their faith. Their passion for what they believed to be right fueled violence and injustice—deeds that would be unthinkable if we did not live in the century when no human cruelty became unthinkable.

William Hathorne reportedly sailed from England on the *Arbella,* one of eleven ships bearing seven hundred passengers, two hundred and forty cows, and sixty horses. Idlers and thieves had been weeded out in advance by agents of the Massachusetts Bay Colony. The voyagers sat on shipboard for two weeks waiting for the wind to be right for sailing. Stepping on board for the three-month trip must have been their first crucial test of faith. William arrived in Naumkeag harbor with dozens of pious and scurvy-weakened Puritans. They brought ballast of bricks and hardware, family chests packed with leather doublets, wool waistcoats, steeple-crowned felt hats, farthingales, stomachers, shoe buckles, a few favorite books, and packets of seed. Among the passengers were Governor John Winthrop, Lady Arbella Johnson (whose financial support helped to launch the New England migration), Sir Richard Saltonstall, Anne and Simon Bradstreet, William Hathorne and his younger brother John and sister Elizabeth. They had endured tempests and contrary winds, during which seamen and passengers alike fasted to earn God's forbearance. In rough seas they were confined below deck for days, the stench of sickness and waste as penetrating as the cold. They called the voyage a baptism. So stern was the Puritan sense of righteousness—excommunication for card playing—that it's difficult to imagine them, even in these circumstances, taking comfort from one another. More likely, sermons and long prayer lulled them, each hardship an opportunity to demonstrate the power of their faith.

I have searched through Puritan writings looking for expressions of vulnerability, fear, or intimacy, wanting to understand the emotional quality of their lives. What afflictions did they suffer that gave them the courage to pull up stakes and head three thousand miles toward the probable ruin of a wilderness existence? The authors don't allow such disclosures, at least not in the letters, journals, sermons, and narratives I've come across. Fallibility and suffering were given, the groundwork of faith, not pathology to be examined. They expressed even marital tenderness through the language of religious belief. In a letter to his wife written while the *Arbella* lay becalmed in port, John Winthrop wrote:

> And now (my sweet soul) I must once again take my last farewell of thee in Old England; it goeth verye near my heart to leaue thee, but I know to whom I haue committed thee euen to him, who loues the(e) much better than any husband can who hath taken account of the haires of thy head, and putts all thy teares in his bottle, who can, and (if it be for his glorye) will bringe us together againe with peace and comfort.

William Hathorne was the oldest and smartest child among seven born to a yeoman family living on ancestral farmlands in Binfield, England. He was raised to work the land, to grow wheat, barley, oats, and hay and tend cattle, sheep, bees, and horses. But the family recognized William's promise at an early age and saw that he got an unusually good education for someone of his class. It served him well. His eloquence, earnestness, and political sense gave him the social mobility of gentry. His favorite book, the one he carried with him on the *Arbella,* was Philip Sidney's *Arcadia,* a pastoral romance about an idealized land. But William's most passionate interest was in religious matters. At the Binfield church, where his family worshiped, the Church of England preaching was vehemently opposed to religious dissent. Puritans, he was taught, were the most traitorous dissenters because of their severe code of discipline and their fervor to rid the Church of England of Roman

Catholicism. But as a teenager, William spent time at his grandfather's farm near Dorchester and there began to hear firsthand
the revolutionary ideology. Reverend John White, a Puritan and
Calvinist, assailed the "popishly addicted" and condemned the
corruption of priests: "In all excess of sin, Papists have been the
ringleaders, in riotous companies, in drunken meetings, in sedi-
tious assemblies & practices, & in profaning the Sabbath, in quar-
rels & brawls in stage plays, greens, ales, & all heathenish
customs."

Convinced that with clear will, plain worship, good deeds, and
strict moral codes they could be one with God, the Puritans set out
to live exemplary lives. They intended to bring Christianity back to
its original humility and communal roots. Theirs was a community
not only of faith, but of radical dissent from moral hypocrisy. For
many of the dissenters, the answer to the ruin that European
Christianity had become was to leave it behind and sow the seeds
of "God's new Plantation" in the American wilderness.

By the time he was twenty-one, William had converted.

Reverend White's followers began to settle in Dorchester,
Massachusetts, in 1628. Among the first was Richard Davenport,
a zealous young disciple who had become a friend of the
Hathornes in England and was engaged to Elizabeth when she was
thirteen years old. A professional soldier, he had been called for
duty in the Massachusetts Bay Colony several years before his
friends and his betrothed were to join him. By the time William,
Elizabeth, and John arrived, Richard had several years of experience with which to guide them. Dorchester was a rough-hewn
town, the homes no more than huts with thatched roofs, mud or
wooden chimneys, and oil-paper windows. For lamps, Reverend
Francis Higginson wrote, they used slices of pine.

> Yea, our pine trees, that are most plentiful of all
> wood, doth allow us plenty of candles, which are
> very useful in a house, and they are such candles
> as the Indians burn, having no other, and they are

> nothing else but wood of the pine tree cloven into
> two little slices, something thin, which are so full
> of the moisture of turpentine and pitch, that they
> burn as clear as a torch.

William had the help of his young brother, John, still a teenager. In the custom of the times, John had papers of indenture to his older brother stipulating that he must work for him until he was eighteen. Prospective settlers had been encouraged to bring young children to the colony, because the children could earn more than the cost of their keep by working in the cornfields. For the Hathorne parents remaining in Binfield, the experience of watching three of their children fall in with the spiritual enemy and then sail off into a perilous self-exile must have been wrenching. Four other children remained in England to continue the farming tradition. The fate of the exiles was unknown to those who stayed at home. When the father made his will, he bequeathed one hundred pounds to William, forty to Elizabeth, and twenty to John, "if not dead."

The settlers endured poverty, epidemic, hurricane, drunken brawling, and a plague of caterpillars, which, it was believed, fell in a great thunder shower and decimated their crops. Nevertheless, the newcomers prospered on the bounty of the native forest and on livestock they raised for trade. With many skilled craftsmen and servants among them, they quickly raised frame-and-clapboard houses. By 1629 a brickworks had been established in nearby Salem (formerly Naumkeag, renamed for the Hebrew word for peace) and the more prosperous citizens built gracious brick homes in the thriving seaport.

Even the most devout wrote with great admiration and earnestness of the "Earth of New England." As Higginson stated: "I will endeavor to show you what New England is ... and truly endeavor, by God's help, to report nothing of New England but what I have partly seen with mine own eyes, and partly heard and inquired from the mouths of very honest and religious persons...." He went on to catalog the "commodities and discommodities" of the land, praising the air, water, and soil; the abundance of native turnips, parsnips, carrots, herbs, pumpkins, mulberries, plums, raspberries, currants, chestnuts, filberts, walnuts, hurtleberries; the varieties of wood—"There is no better in the world"; and the beasts—some bears, lions, several sorts of deer, "some whereof bring three or four young ones at once, which is not ordinary in England; also wolves, foxes, beavers, otters, martens, great wild cats, and a great beast called a molke, as big as an ox." Of the discommodities, Higginson cited mosquitoes, the cold winter season, and "snakes and serpents, of strange colors and huge greatness. Yea there are some serpents, called rattlesnakes, that have rattles in their tails, that will not fly from a man as others will, but will fly upon him and sting him so mortally that he will die within a quarter of an hour after, except the party stinged have about him some of the root of an herb called snake-weed to bite on, and then he shall receive no harm." And finally, among the discommodities he cited: "here wants as yet the good company of honest Christians ... to make use of this fruitful land. Great pity is to see so much good ground for corn, and for grass as any is under the heavens, to lie altogether unoccupied, when so many honest men and their families in Old England, through populousness thereof, do make very hard shift to live one by the other."

Puritans wrote descriptions of how to make sugar from maple sap, how to find where the bees hive in the woods and how to collect their honey; they wrote field notes on berries, oaks, and fish, and sent specimens to England for further study. The writing shows intelligence, an appreciation for complexity, attention to the thing itself, praise for nature's generative power, and careful detail: "seeds found in the gizzards of wild-fowl which afterwards sprouted in the Earth." Even Cotton Mather, pastor at the North Church in Boston, who is remembered for his pedantic, intolerant, and oppressive vigor, wrote about nature with an inquiring scientific eye—at times also with wonder and love. In his essay "On Vegetables," he wrote:

How unaccountably is the *Figure* of *Plants* preserved? And how unaccountably their *Growth*
determined? Our excellent *Ray* [John Ray, a pioneer in English natural history] flies to an intelligent *plastick Nature,* which must understand and
regulate the whole Oeconomy. Every particular
part of the *Plant* has its astonishing Uses. The
Roots give it a Stability, and fetch the Nourishment into it, which lies in the Earth ready for it.
The *Fibres* contain and convey the Sap which carries up that Nourishment. The *Plant* has also
larger Vessels, which entertain the proper and
specifick Juice of it; and others to carry the Air for
its necessary respiration. The outer and inner
Bark defend it from Annoyances, and contribute
to its Augmentation. The *Leaves* embrace and
preserve the *Flower* and *Fruit* as they come to
their explication ... How agreeable the *Shade* of
Plants, let every Man say that *sits under his own
Vine, and under his own Fig-tree!* How charming
the Proportion and Pulchritude of the *Leaves,* the
Flowers, the *Fruits,* he who confesses not, must
be, as Dr. *More* says, *one sunk into a forlorn pitch
of Degeneracy, and stupid as a Beast.*

Sooner or later, all Puritan writing returns to faith; all praise of
nature becomes an invitation to praise God. The historians—those
who would master the conflicting stories of the past and tell the
definitive tale—say that for the Puritans wilderness was not a place
to encounter the sacred, but a place of inherent evil, a moral empti-
ness where they could be tested and prove themselves as worthy
as saints. Contemporary historian Perry Miller writes that "the
Puritan felt that unless he could see the divine purpose in the
phenomenal world he had failed to interpret his facts correctly.
For him nature was a revelation of the divine order which had
pre-existed in the mind of God before it was incarnated in matter,
and its highest value was symbolic."

I find the stories muddled and contradictory, replete with fearful references to "the howling wilderness," reverent submission to God's will as the primary survival skill, as well as an unmistakable sensual engagement with nature, at times a rapturous love of natural beauty, and the scientific intelligence (in 1721!) to inoculate the population of Boston against smallpox. The hope that I could understand the Puritans' relationship with the American wilderness and how their beliefs shaped that relationship now seems overreaching. Like us, the Puritans were inconsistent, conflicted and complex, driven by hopes they could not realize.

Without people, wilderness asks for no value or meaning—it simply is. The values and meanings that people project onto the blank screen of the wild become the ground on which their relationship with nature is played out. If the wilderness is evil, we subdue it. If it is sacred, we go there to feed the soul. If wilderness is all we mean when we say "nature," then we suffer an alienation from the various forces that spawn, sustain, and limit us. I have always been taken by the sheer sensuality of the North American continent. Wild water sculpting flows and basins into rock, the dense profusion of all-terrain greenery that gentles the pitch of rocky land, the shocking and delicate appearance of flower genitals in the woods—May beauties, trout lilies, wild orchids, and the scrotal pouch of the lady's slipper. Even snow can turn the harshest land into a contour smooth as airbrushed skin. And the animals—lynx, fox, elk, moose, mustang, cougar, river otter, porpoise, hare—each name conjuring a specific liquid movement, the self-possessed physicality with which they kill, eat, breed, and wash. I sleep with two cats and the touch of their fur brushing against my naked skin is among the most beautiful sensations I can think of. They calm me, these animals who could be wild but choose not to be, who go outside to kill and lounge around, then come home every day for the food I provide and for my touch. They bridge me over to that animal country from which I came, a place in which the body poses no questions, only needs.

I go to the wilderness for spiritual comfort, to get away from the demands placed on me, and to feel closer to the mystery of the big biological enterprise in which I'm a small part. I don't hunt—though I'd like to give it a try—I fish only occasionally and eat the catch more for pleasure than need. In the woods I harvest only wild berries and chanterelles—both luxury items that have more to do with delight than with survival. I go to the city for my physical needs—food, clothing, books, hardware, friends, and sometimes for the sexiness of the city itself.

That I experience the wilderness as the nexus between sensuality and spirituality is a comfort to me. My ancestors, I suspect, experienced that nexus as a torment. Their entire subsistence came from the woods. They arrived thinking faith was their sanctuary, not the land. Yet everywhere they looked for spirit, they found confounding matter. They feared snakes, bears, wolves, and mythic animals that settlers swore they had seen—"lions and serpentlike monsters with two heads." Though game birds, deer, and firewood were more plentiful than in England, and herring so abundant that they learned from the Indians how to "fish the fields" (burying the catch as they tilled the soil) to fertilize their corn, subsistence remained an iffy proposition. Every early settler's experience of America had to have been one of grueling physicality where progress meant mastering the material world in order to survive. Many winter nights they must have sat out a gale, backdrafts of smoke leaking from the mud-and-stick chimney, taking cold comfort from cracked Indian corn boiled in seawater.

The English came from a populated country where patches of woods and heath were surrounded by settled farms, towns, and cities. They arrived in a place where fragile settlements were surrounded by enormous unmapped woods. The only roads were Indian footpaths leading from nowhere to nowhere. The "salvages" (from the Latin *silva*, woods) burned their villages behind them, leaving little trace of where they had made habitation. In England the Puritans called the outlaws who ranged in Windsor Forest "the Devil's children." They did not mean it as a metaphor.

In America some argued that the Indians should be compensated for the lands the Massachusetts Bay Colony was granting to settlers. To the devout, the notion was outrageous. "The earth is the Lord's and the fullness thereof; to the saints is the earth given; we are the saints."

William Hathorne initially settled in Dorchester and rose quickly to a position of respect and prominence as a selectman and a member of the General Court. Among his duties were writing laws and determining damages in disputes between neighbors over livestock and crops. Life in the colony was hard work, which is just what he wanted—only through discipline could the faithful bring about God's new Plantation. William had contempt for those who idled, lied, or failed to conform. His totem biblical verses came from Genesis—the story of God punishing those who break the rules. Stocks and whipping posts were set up in town and he continued the customary English methods of punishment—branding, flogging, stocking, cutting off ears. Many Puritans acted out their faith with a heretical flare, defacing images of Catholic saints, naming their children Experience, Hopestill, Desire, and Supply. William's sister Elizabeth and her husband, Richard Davenport, named their first child Truecross, in honor of John Endecott's dramatic act of defiance at Salem. Ensign Davenport had been drilling his band of citizen soldiers on the town common when Endecott rode onto the scene, grabbed Davenport's standard and with the flash of his sword cut from the fabric the image of Saint George's cross, which he considered a symbol of popery. William was more traditional, naming his first daughter Sarah, and turning his attention increasingly to public discipline. In 1636, he moved to Salem where he became county judge and where the family was to flourish for five generations. In addition to his magisterial duties, he became heavily involved in trade, building a wharf and warehouse to store his "adventures."

By midcentury Salem had three thousand residents—mostly fishermen, farmers, shipbuilders, shopkeepers, and indentured servants. There were also thirty or forty Black slaves whom the Puritans had brought on ships and sold in the open market. After the Pequot War of 1637, dozens of Indian captives were shipped to the West Indies to be sold into slavery. A girl branded +110- on the belly was acquired by Richard Davenport. In the burgeoning theocracy, ministers were the most respected citizens, and after them magistrates, whose duties included serving as trial judge, moral arbiter, director of police, prosecutor, and supervisor of informers sent to search for criminals. The accused had no defense counsel. They had to plead their own cases before the magistrate, whose judgments were considered infallible. Because the Massachusetts Bay Colony was a theocracy, by law only church members were allowed to vote (this amounted to about one in every five adult males). It also meant that a sin was considered a crime, and punished as such.

A man who had filched "soap to wash his shirts" and another who had pilfered "half a cheese, a cake, and some milk" were caught by informers. For punishment they had to pay restitution of twice the value of the goods, take a public whipping, and wear the letter *T* on their clothing for a month. William Hathorne once ordered a constable to cut off a convicted burglar's ear and brand the letter *B* on his forehead. If babies were born too soon after marriage, the mothers were sentenced to whipping and fines. Citizens were fined for failing to attend church on the Sabbath, for "speaking slightingly and scornfully" of the minister, or for mocking Christian practices as did a man from Salem who declared, "Next year I'll be a member of the church and have my dog christened." Adultery, rape, and sodomy could be tried as capital crimes. A man and a woman found "not guilty of adultery but of very suspicious acts leading to adultery" were sentenced to stand for an hour on the gallows with ropes around their necks and then to be tied to a cart and whipped while they were driven through the streets of Boston and Charlestown.

The importance placed on discipline and conformity is even

clearer in the story of Mary Oliver, whose desire to worship according to her own conscience was considered heretical. In England she had been imprisoned for refusing to bow at the naming of Jesus during prayers. In the colony she was sent to jail for asking permission during church to take communion though she was not a church member. Only members were allowed to participate in the sacraments. When brought to General Court, she quoted scripture at length in her own defense, offered no penitence, and was sent back to jail. She won the sympathy of Governor Winthrop by admitting she had done wrong to disturb the church service and was released. Within a year she was back in jail, this time for criticizing the church and government within earshot of immigrants newly arrived in Salem. She was sentenced to be whipped and Winthrop reported that "she stood without tieing, and bore her punishment with a masculine spirit, glorying in her sufferings." For six years she continued to appeal for church membership, but with no success. In bitter defiance, she declaimed to an informer, "All the ministers in this country are blood-thirsty men. My blood is too thin for them to draw it out." She was sent back to court, sentenced to stand tied to the whipping post for three hours with a slit stick pinched over her tongue. The punishment served only to sharpen her criticism of Hathorne. "I do hope to live and tear his flesh in pieces, and all such as he." The battle heated. She was in and out of court for working on the Sabbath, living apart from her husband, defamation, petty theft—a barrage of actual and trumped-up infractions. She in turn brought charges of brutality against the constable, for which she was granted restitution of ten shillings, and did not cease to speak her mind. The twelve-year feud ended, talk brewing that she might be a witch, with her banishment to England in 1651. She died shortly thereafter.

There were other responses to the new land by those who came for the wealth in lumber and furs. And by those for whom the body of the land awoke a sensual engagement, inheritors of ancient wild revelry. They dressed in animal masks, skins, and horns, threading flowers into their hair and clothing, dancing in the forest with Indians, and drinking the fermented fruits of the harvest. Some settled in the town of Mount Wollaston and, in the medieval English custom, erected a maypole eighty feet tall with a pair of buck's horns nailed on top. Aroused by a barrel of excellent beer, they danced, weaving streamers and garlands around the pole. They changed the name of the town to Merry Mount. By William Bradford's account, the settlement "fell to great licentiousness," with Thomas Morton, an Anglican who had come to the colony in 1625 to set up fur trade, as the Lord of Misrule. Morton "composed sundry rhymes and verses, some tending to lasciviousness, and others to the detraction and scandal of some persons, which he affixed to this idle or idol maypole." This irreverence brought censure in the form of John Endecott and a company of soldiers (likely Lieutenant Davenport among them), who dispersed the rowdies, cut down the maypole, consigned the pagans to stocks and whipping posts, and deported Morton temporarily back to England.

There was Anne Hutchinson of Boston, who believed that salvation could be won by faith and had nothing to do with good works. She defied the Puritan fathers by holding weekly gatherings in her home. Sixty or more people would regularly come to hear her lecture. She was tried in General Court and sentenced to banishment for "traducing the ministers." And there was Reverend Roger Williams, for a time minister in Salem, a Puritan who believed in "the liberty of conscience"—that civil magistrates could have no power over matters of individual conscience, that there was room in the righteous heart for many faiths. He befriended the Indians, often serving as mediator when disputes flared. He was tried for heresy. William Hathorne voted for his banishment.

When discontent and protest grew among the people, the theocrats saw it as Satan's work—their Plantation in danger of being uprooted and an occasion to strengthen their resolve by enforcing morally correct behavior. Word came from overseas about the Friends, new radicals of the faith community in England, who believed in a doctrine of direct revelation and equality of all before God. They had no ministers and took their hats off to no one. Because the Friends believed in honoring the commandment "Thou shalt not kill" in the strictest sense, any war was considered unrighteous. Those who came to the colony believed that American land rightly belonged to the Indians. Such freethinkers were not welcome in Massachusetts. They were flogged and holes were burned through their tongues with hot irons. They were hounded, banished, and hanged. Still they continued to arrive and to make converts of many Puritans, some of whom had been Hathorne's close friends. His own son John married a Quaker. The court tried to tighten its control by keeping out newcomers, establishing fines for hosting strangers in one's home. In an order to a constable, Hathorne wrote, "You are required, by virtue hereof, to search in all suspicious places for private meetings; and if they refuse to open the doors, you are to break open the door upon them, and return the names of those you find." But in 1660, Charles II was restored to the English throne and the Puritan theocracy in New England collapsed. After four Quakers had been hung in Boston, the monarch ruled that all cases against Friends would be tried in England.

Initially relations with the Indians had been peaceful, if only because the Puritans saw the locals as a source of food, and as potential converts—an essential aspect of their work in God's Plantation. As John Hooker had written during the Pequot War, "Only rebel ye not against the Lord, neither fear ye the people of the land; for they are bread for us: their defence is departed from them, & the Lord is with us: fear them not." Cotton Mather espoused this view more tenaciously than most, writing as late as the 1690s:

> The Natives of the Country now Possessed by the
> *New-Englanders,* had been forlorn and wretched
> *Heathen* ever since their first herding here; and

> tho' we know not *When* or *How* those *Indians*
> first became Inhabitants of this mighty Continent,
> yet we may guess that probably the Devil decoy'd
> those miserable Salvages hither, in hopes that the
> Gospel of the Lord Jesus Christ would never come
> here to destroy or disturb his *Absolute Empire*
> over them.

The Pequot War had ended in a thirty-eight-year peace with the Indians and many settlers believed that the native people would be made "faithful subjects of the King of God's State." And it seems many were—there were reportedly fourteen villages of Praying Indians in Massachusetts in 1674. Just what their conversion entailed is unclear. Mary Rowlandson wrote about seeing a Praying Indian who wore "a string about his neck, strung with Christians' fingers." When war with the Indians broke out again in 1675, Hathorne's reading of the text was predictable: "Jehovah in the wrath of his vengeance is scowling upon you, and not again will He show His smile until you return to the paths of godliness which your fathers trod." His solution was to make stricter laws: any man who wore a periwig would be fined. A "Day of Publick Humiliation, with fasting and prayer" was ordered throughout the colony. But the people, now second- and third-generation New Englanders, saw the war differently: "God is angry, and is chastising all of us for the blood the ministers and magistrates spilled in persecuting such as the Quakers."

One of the most remarkable books of the war period is Mary Rowlandson's narrative of being held captive among the Indians for nearly twelve weeks. It offers a day-by-day account of tribal life through a Puritan's eyes, a vivid sense of her biblical learning and devotion, records of savagery by all parties—both sides eagerly slaughtering, scalping, burning towns and crops, smashing babies' heads, taking and selling slaves—records of exhaustion and remorse, and insight into how profoundly the Puritans believed that God intended the wilderness for the elect alone. Fleeing from the English army, Rowlandson's captors came on a Friday to the Bacquaug River. The Indians quickly cut trees and fashioned rafts to cross over. There were a great number in the party—so many that Rowlandson could not count them—so the crossing took until Sunday night. Provisions were scant. While waiting for the remaining members of the tribe to join them, Rowlandson's band "boyled an old Horses leg which they had got, and so we drank the broth, as soon as they thought it was ready, and when it almost all gone, they filled it up again." It was the third week of her captivity and food she had thought to be "filthy trash" she had learned to savor. And her view of the moral nature of Indians was clear:

> And here I cannot but take notice of the strange providence of God in preserving the heathen: They were many hundreds, old and young, some sick, and some lame, many had Papooses at their backs, the greatest number at this time with us, were Squaws, and they travelled with all they had, bag and baggage, and yet they got over this River aforesaid; and on Munday they set their Wigwams on fire, and away they went: On that very day came the English Army after them to this River, and saw the smoak of their Wigwams, and yet this River put a stop to them. God did not give them courage or activity to go over after us; we were not ready for so great a mercy as victory and deliverance; if we had been, God would have found out a way for the English to have passed this River, as well as for the Indians with their Squaws and Children, and all their Luggage.

One might read into such an experience not the unworthiness of one's own people, but the apparently greater worth in God's eyes of the Indians. But such a possibility was not available to the Puritan imagination. At the end of her captivity, when reflecting upon "a few remarkable passages of providence" and on the remarkable survival skills of her captors, Rowlandson wrote:

It was thought, if their Corn were cut down, they would starve and dy with hunger: and all their Corn that could be found, was destroyed, and they driven from that little they had in store, into the Woods in the midst of Winter; and yet how to admiration did the Lord preserve them for his holy ends, and the destruction of many still amongst the English! strangely did the Lord provide for them; that I did not see (all the time I was among them) one Man, Woman, or Child, die of hunger.

Though many times they would eat that, that a Hog or a Dog would hardly touch; yet by that God strengthened them to be a scourge to his People.

The chief and commonest food was Ground-nuts: They eat also Nuts and Acorns, Harty-choaks, Lilly roots, Ground-beans, and several other weeds and roots, that I know not.

They would pick up old bones, and cut them to pieces at the joynts, and if they were full of wormes and magots, they would scald them over the fire to make the vermine come out, and then boile them, and drink up the Liquor, and then beat the great ends of them in a Morter, and so eat them. They would eat Horses guts, and ears, and all sorts of wild Birds which they could catch: also Bear, Vennison, Beaver, Tortois, Frogs, Squirrels, Dogs, Skunks, Rattle-snakes; yea, the very Bark of Trees; besides all sorts of creatures, and provision they plundered from the English. I can but stand in admiration to see the wonderful power of God, in providing for such a vast number of our Enemies in the Wilderness, where there was nothing to be seen, but from hand to mouth. Many times in a morning, the generality of them would eat up all they had, and yet have some forther supply against they wanted. It is said, Psal. 81. 13,14. *Oh that my People had hearkened to me, and Israel had walked in my ways, I should soon have subdued their Enemies, and turned my*

hand against their Adversaries. But now our perverse and evil carriages in the sight of the Lord,
have so offended him, that instead of turning his
hand against them, the Lord feeds and nourishes
them up to be a scourge to the whole Land.

The moral tyranny with which William Hathorne earned his
respect and prominence did not end with his death in 1681. His
son John was educated in the Puritan school of moral discipline.
He knew his enemies to be Indians, Quakers, Cavaliers warring in
England against the Puritans, the pope and his idolatrous followers, and anyone who spoke against the rules. Unlike his father, who
had renounced the religious tradition in which he'd been raised
(converting from the Church of England to Puritanism) to live out
a vision of spiritual renewal, John accepted the tradition in which
he was raised. His piety was enforced at rigorous Sabbath services
lasting all day. The passionate liturgy imprinted upon him a vis-
ceral terror of God's censure. A treatise by Thomas Hooker titled
The Soul's Preparation for Christ might set the tone of John
Hathorne's childhood:

First, judge the lion by his paw, judge the torments of hell by some little beginning of it; and
the dregs of God's vengeance, by some little sips
of it; and judge how unable thou art to bear the
whole by thy inability to bear a little of it in this
life, in the terror of conscience ... Conceive thus
much, if all the diseases in the world did seize on
one man, and if all torments that all the tyrants
of the world could devise, were cast upon him;
and if all the creatures in heaven and earth did
conspire the destruction of this man; and if all the
devils in hell did labor to inflict punishments
upon him; you would think this man to be in a
miserable condition. And yet all this is but a beam
of God's indignation. If the beams of God's wrath
be so hot, what is the full sun of his wrath, when
it shall seize upon the soul of a sinful creature in
full measure?

John Hathorne believed the death penalty was suitable punishment for religious heresy. At the age of forty-three he became a Salem magistrate.

Witchcraft had troubled Europe since the fourteenth century. During the Spanish Inquisition, instituted by Ferdinand and Isabella, as many as a hundred accused witches had been burned in a single day: a carnival, with vendors hawking food, souvenirs, and rosaries. Executions peaked in the sixteenth and seventeenth centuries. Thousands, mostly women, were executed in England, Scotland, and the rest of Europe, accused of signing agreements with the Devil in exchange for supernatural powers. Even Francis Bacon, the father of empiricism, apparently believed in witchcraft. In retrospect, it seems grandly ironic that the religion based on two supernatural events—a virgin birth and resurrection of the dead—should find the mere suspicion of such powers to be its most dangerous enemy.

Although the witch-killing frenzy did not ignite in Massachusetts until 1692, the hanging forty years earlier of Ann Hibbins in Boston and Margaret Jones in Charlestown as witches had prepared the ground. Witchcraft was the worst of capital crimes—worse than murder, rape, or arson. It marked a crisis for the colony—the Devil retaking His land. The witch trials in Salem were conducted in the meetinghouse, where worship services also were held. Sentences came down accompanied by sermons. Some accounts say that John Hathorne was the most fervent and least repentant judge, others that he merely conducted the preliminary hearings. It's known that from June until October more than one hundred of the accused appeared before him. Twenty were executed—five hanged at one time. Dozens waited in jail either for trial or execution, several dying there from hunger and cold, until public outcry and a reprieve from the governor stopped the persecutions.

Prepared the ground ... that's what they did, these accomplished ancestors who, in the name of God, inflicted two generations of eloquent, dictatorial, systematized, and self-righteous cruelty upon their neighbors. What did I hope to claim in examining these lives? What is there to honor in these elders? What obligation do I have to their story? What taint do I carry in my blood? I don't intend to claim any privilege here in my ancestry—we've all got some of this poison in our veins—heirs to slaughtering, torture, persecution, and injustice. So broadly rooted and branching is any family tree, who could claim to be free of this wretched aspect of the past? As Benjamin Sáenz has written, "American history is sordid and bloody and disgusting, and nothing will ever convince me that our national past has been heroic." This continent in its openness seemed to invite a particularly virulent form of greeting—a misapprehension on the part of our ancestors for which we who follow owe the land some tenderness.

My father used to joke that we had Indian blood—related to Pocahontas was how he told it. He usually said this when he was lost on back roads trying to find a new shortcut, a practice he preferred to highway frenzy. Americans love to play Indian—not the actual poverty and depletion of reservation living, but the dream of living wild, innocent, defiant, and free—in touch with the sacred powers of the land. Who wants to say, I've got Indian-killer blood, slave-trader blood, witch-hanger and tyrant blood? What would one do with this history? One cannot uproot it, but one can make it show itself. One can lament the suffering they caused. One can say that William and John Hathorne, out of blindness and good intentions, brought shame to our family. One can remember the words of Solomon Stoddard, born in Boston in 1643, who wrote this in *Concerning Ancestors:*

> The mistakes of one generation many times become the calamity of succeeding generations. The present generation are not only unhappy by reason of the darkness of their own minds, but the errors of those who have gone before them have been a foundation of a great deal of misery.

> Posterity is very prone to espouse the principles of
> ancestors, and from an inordinate veneration of
> them to apprehend a sacredness in their opinions,
> and don't give themselves the trouble to make an
> impartial examination of them—as if it were a
> transgression to call them into question, and bor-
> dered upon irreligion to be wavering about them
> ... And if any particular persons have been led by
> God into the understanding of those mistakes,
> and have made their differing sentiments public,
> it has proved an occasion of much sorrow; and
> many people have fallen into parties, whereby a
> spirit of love has been quenched and great heats
> have risen, from whence have proceeded censures
> and reproaches, and sometimes separation and
> persecution.

What would one ask of such ancestors—so pious and articulate,
so educated and dedicated to the common good, so committed to
a better future for humankind? *How could you have been so blind?*
And they would answer, *Because of our faith.* What would they
ask of us? *Don't be faithless.* We would scoff, *What is faith?* They
would reply, *The possibility of our goodness.* Wise and frightened
ancestors, tell me this: *If faith blinds, makes us cold to another's
suffering, must we be faithless to see?*

WOODS WORK

A PHOTOGRAPH OF AN EMPTY HOUSE. WEATHERED clapboards, two and a half stories, a simple peaked rectangular box, windows and doors gone, the interior open to the wind. On the roof, a foot of snow; in the dooryard, a three-foot drift. A few weedy blackberry canes poke through the white crust. Worn and leaning cedar fence posts run along the south wall. The neighbor's cows have been grazing where once a clothesline hung, where a garden of purple iris and oriental poppies made an annual spectacle. In the background, ice-blue sky. Two leafless apple trees, which, untended, have lost their shapeliness. The deadwood is tangled with a snarl of overgrown suckers, the bark scarred with woodpecker holes and burly scabs left from limb falls. In the foreground, a narrow dirt road packed hard with snow, overlapping lines of wheel-track where a few cars and the milk truck have passed. I stood across the road and snapped the picture from my yard.

That ruin was so beautiful to me it might have been the statue of a fallen god. I contemplated the varied patina of aging wood, the damaged fancywork under eaves and over the front door. I never walked inside because the floors, rotted through, had caved into the cellarhole. In the rubble one could see the remains of a lost domestic order—broken skeleton of a cast-iron cookstove, crockery shards, barrel staves, zinc-lidded canning jars, rags of clothing and feedsacks, battered sap buckets, and bullet-punctured tin cans. Whoever the ghost neighbors were who had left this junk behind, they called up the America I wanted, a country where everyone was a farmer, no matter what else they did; a country where everyone lived next to nowhere and had to figure out from scratch how to make the land provide; a country where one could shape the future with the ache of one's own labor.

I moved to that borderland just south of the Canadian line in the winter of 1969, when my daughter was three years old and I was twenty-two. Vermont, until then, had meant playland to me. I skied there, often with free passes my father had gotten from advertisers on his radio or television shows. At one mountain I'd walk into the manager's office, tell him whose daughter I was, and walk out with a weekend pass for myself and my boyfriend of the moment. Our family had driven north to a Vermont resort one summer. I don't remember much about the trip. We must have gone swimming and played tennis and taken walks in the woods. What I do remember is that the owners had a dog who had just come home from the animal hospital. They'd made an entertaining joke out of the dog's experience; they'd ask him about his opera- tion, coaxing a little, until he began to bay and whine. Then every- one would laugh at how smart the dog was, understanding so many words; how cute that he remembered his pain. Again and again, as new guests arrived, the loving owners put the little canine through his performance. Again and again, everyone laughed lov- ingly, exchanging knowing looks. That was the summer when the adult world began to look a bit perverse to me. And once, several years later, during the Summer of Love I had come to Vermont for a weekend with members of my tribe for a planned acid trip in the fern meadows of an isolated section of woods near Killington. That was the summer that planted some seed in my mind that grew into my moving north.

By then I had scandalized my family by dropping out of college, five months pregnant. I had endured and escaped a short and dis- mal forced marriage, committing myself to an extent I did not yet understand to an experimental life. Much of the experiment had to do with sex. I was unconvinced by fifties propriety in sexual matters—that Doris Day dream of feminine resistance against the Rock Hudson hounding of male seduction. I'd read enough great literature, seen enough Gilbert and Sullivan, Shakespeare and O'Neill—books and theater bestowed on me by parents who hoped to protect me from the evils of popular culture—to know that human passion was a mystery too complicated to be understood by ignoring it. In fumbling teenage attempts at intimacy, I learned fast that the body's responses are not contingent upon the heart or the head. That seemed good—a capacity to celebrate, not curtail. Erich Fromm's book *The Art of Loving* was passing among students like the flu. From it I got the idea that the shame of Adam and Eve was caused not by sex, but by their separateness, by the man and the woman remaining strangers to each other. One thing the sexes had in common was desire. It seemed a place to meet. In high school I admired an older couple (they must have been nineteen) who were openly sexual. Driving around with them one day, I was stunned to see her nestle her hand into his crotch and keep it there even though she knew I had noticed. That openness seemed a thing to strive for. I vowed to myself that the first time I went all the way would be intentional, loving, and unashamed—not a backseat fumble in which the lamb succumbed to the wolf.

But sex, like death, is hard to plan for, no matter what one wants or knows. I stumbled into what I hadn't planned on, got lost in the headlong sensations that a certain good-time boy could bring me to. We were seventeen and the only thing serious about the time we spent together was our passion. We may not have been particularly intelligent, or even in love, but at least we taught each other a thing or two about the pleasure our bodies were capable of. For that, I'm grateful. Our daughter was born on March 21, 1965, the spring after I had graduated from high school.

We spent a few years in Cambridge before the teenage marriage came apart; my husband and brother were students at Boston University. I had everything to prove about being a parent and I knew it. The guys got into psychedelics. Leary and Alpert had just been fired from Harvard. Before that no one had heard of hallucinogens. The drug talk was everywhere—"a structural regression of the ego ... more in line with Zen thinking ... mystic states as the function of a flexible ego." People tried blotter, buttons, and speed, as if each were a new album by the Stones. The streets were boiling. There was a cadre of us by then—a circle of tight friends, the circumference as permeable as a cell membrane. Many circles like that. Tribal parties of long-hairs, we met and trusted each other by signs. Weed, hair, clothes weren't fashion, but code to identify cultural revolutionaries working to make life our religion and our art. I read *Summerhill: A Radical Approach to Child Rearing* and began to take motherhood seriously. To love well, for fallible creatures, was a radical act. I felt frightened and exhilarated by the challenge.

My daughter and I ended up settling near the Cold Hollow Mountains, the largest unbroken range in Vermont, situated twenty miles south of the Canadian border. Dairy farm and maple syrup country. Some logging. Much poverty. I worked as a dishwasher at a ski resort—no longer the manager's darling. But there I began to meet other urban refugees who had settled in the hills. Our arrival predated the back-to-the-land movement: more farms were abandoned than working. Land could be bought for two hundred dollars an acre. I owned one savings bond worth a thousand dollars, which my grandmother had given me. With it I made the down payment on a house, barn, and three and a half acres of cleared land on a dirt road. In one direction, I looked out at the forested bowl of mountains where snow could last until July; in the other, at the large empty clapboard house gone to ruin. Our house, not a ruin, was just a dump. In the cellar snored a dinosaur of an old wood furnace used for central heat. There was no bathroom to speak of, a toilet in a closet when we started out; no insulation, no television, no phone. But families had lived this way for decades and I figured so could we.

The first frost came by Labor Day, the last at the end of May. In winter, weeks passed when the mercury didn't climb over zero—the snow and wind grew fierce. Nights fell to twenty, thirty below. In the deepest cold, nothing moved but smoke from the chimneys. Snow packed on the dirt road creaked under foot or wheels. In the gone-by orchard the trees were frozen stiff, icy twig tips clicking in the wind, chimes made of bones. The air itself seemed frozen. In the neighbor's barn, steam heat rose off the backs of stanchioned cows, their breath making warm clouds as they nuzzled in their grain—animals large enough, and enough of them, to keep their own space warm. I worked hard at it—splitting and hauling wood, wearing heavy woolen socks to bed. When pipes froze, I learned to use a blowtorch. Outside the bedroom window, the moon ran its light through giant icicles hanging from the roof. I thought they looked like glass teeth, as if I were trying to sleep inside the mouth of a beast.

In the miserably short summer, I grew gorgeous gardens—never perfectly tended, but productive nonetheless. I froze and canned vegetables, made cider and sauerkraut, dried herbs, raised hens and pigs. Like a cover photo for *Organic Gardening* magazine, I stood beaming knee-deep in comfrey, showing off a cabbage two feet wide, my cheeks as smooth as a butternut squash. I was home. Nothing makes one feel at home, and stay at home, like keeping animals and growing gardens. I was happy in my hardship. I built a desk out of barnboards in the living room, stripped the walls to find, under the plaster and lath, planking three feet wide. I brushed the rough-cut surface with linseed oil to heighten the grain. My daughter Lucinda's room was sprawled with Leggos, Tonkas, Playdoh, broken Crayolas, stuffed and plastic animals, a dripping easel and scattered sheets torn from jumbo newsprint pads. The gone-wild territory of her playing became a sovereign nation with a culture so ingrained it could not be suppressed with my cheerful colonizing dictum, "Time to clean up your room." There was much I could not give her. Yet I felt certain that she'd be all right if I gave her love as bedrock and the skill to deal with change. Nights I'd lie awake in bed, listening to the deep clarity and silence of the north. I'd listen to my heart and wonder if it was all right. When a lady from the church brought us a gift basket of fruit and nuts for Thanksgiving, I realized that we were poor.

I had come for the woods, not merely to live with a view of green felted hills, but to be nestled into that leafy profusion. The northeast woods, not grand, not intimidating like in the West, are comforting—the mountains old and worn, thickly green with second-growth forest. A century ago the Vermont hills had been a solid patchwork quilt of farms, houses dotting the tended pastures and meadows, hedgerows and a few marker trees growing along the fencelines. When I lived there, the forest had claimed back the majority of the farmland; stone walls marked former boundary lines even in the densest woods; weedy roadbeds once used for logging and sugaring made the backcountry accessible. A mile in, one might find an overgrown cellarhole, the yard marked by huge maples and a single black walnut tree, a rose garden taken over by ragweed, daylilies tangled with timothy. In my own neighborhood there had been a sawmill, tannery, schoolhouse, and a Poor Farm with a barracks-like dormitory—all now vacant and ramshackle. The town had started in 1800, population thirty-six, and by 1859 had peaked at fifteen hundred. Much of the land was clear-cut during those sixty years, white pine six feet across logged off. The tallest and straightest trees went to ship builders; much of the rest were cut in segments and smoldered underground to make charcoal for industrial England. "The Iron Age was necessarily a Wood Age too," wrote Eric Sloane, "for our forests were stripped to make charcoal, then the only smelting fuel." What lumber remained was used for local building, or burned for potash, which was leached out and rendered into soap. French Canadians and Irish refugees had come to settle, raised turkeys and cows, banded together to drive them two hundred miles to market in Boston. And almost just as quickly the population had drained away.

Many left to join the gold rush in the West; many died in the Civil War. In 1970, the population just over six hundred, someone painted on the broad side of a barn, BAKERSFIELD CLOSED DUE TO LACK OF INTEREST. Those who remained were either families who had accumulated land wealth by working a farm for several generations or those too poor and discouraged to try again somewhere else.

The maple trees generally fared better than the evergreens, since they produced a lucrative cash crop while alive. For two months of backbreaking woods work in the spring, a family could earn a large portion of its annual income from selling maple syrup. Without that crop, most of the farms would have long since gone the way of the sawmill and tannery. A tended sugarbush makes elegant woods; competing trees thinned out, the crowns of maple spread wide into the open space, making a canopy that shelters the ground. Underneath, islands of shoulder-high ferns proliferate and the leaf mold sends forth a scattering of trout lilies, trillium, and spring beauties—ephemeral blooms always a gift in rough terrain.

What I hadn't planned on during the quiet first years of that decade was community. Musicians, artists, writers, and scientists who'd left college or careers to strip down to essentials were setting up homesteads back in the hills. They bought up ramshackle places, cleared backlots, threw work parties and pig roasts when they needed help raising beams and walls. They turned barns into houses and houses into barns. They jammed, playing blues and bluegrass with the locals, got hired on farms, or a few with the means did the hiring. One musician, a high-school band director, had been fired because he taught the students to play "Sergeant Pepper's Lonely Hearts Club Band." A zoologist kept seagulls in his haybarn, thinking he might get around to completing his dissertation—something about how the red spot on a herring gull's beak is a code telling their babies where to peck for food. There were other children being raised in free-spirited households and communes. One group called themselves the Dreamers. They used to visit the local family planning clinic to get free condoms, which they used for air locks on jugs of home-brew. There were the ones we called "the bad hippies" who stole the firewood out of our yard; a Catholic priest who'd left the church to marry a Cherokee social worker; a woman who'd lived in an urban feminist collective and left to marry a leftist pediatrician who had worked the medical tents at the Democratic Convention in Chicago. Dreamers all, and we kept dreaming. We started a parent cooperative school, a natural foods co-op, a madrigal group, a sitting meditation circle, jug bands, jazz bands, and farming collectives. And there was visiting, lots of laid-back unannounced visiting over coffee and joints, while the children and the music played on. There were games of hide-and-seek in the woods, adults and children playing together; there were love affairs and domestic rearrangements. Everyone seemed to have time for this sociability, though most of us had no money. No one had moved there for a job. That was the point. To take time into our own hands, to rethink our lives right down to their family and economic basis.

In the early seventies, War on Poverty money began to flow into the county and a number of us found work on the public dollar. After having done time as a dishwasher, waitress, farm worker, linotype operator, and free-school teacher, I got hired to be a family planning worker for the clinic opening in the county seat. We set up shop once a month in the hallway and emergency room of a small hospital. The doctors and staff were volunteers. Not until 1972 were unmarried women legally eligible for contraception. Abortion was available only in New York. The clinic was controversial, but Christian fundamentalists had not yet started picketing, harassing patients, or bombing medical facilities. Much of the clinic's public rhetoric spoke of poverty and "family planning." We were morally defensive, citing the neediest case histories—a Catholic woman who'd had fourteen pregnancies by the age of twenty-nine, who had nine living children, an unemployed farm worker for a husband, and a physician ethically opposed to con-traception. But the majority of the patients were single women and many were teenagers. Though we couldn't say so publicly, most of the clinic workers believed these women were entitled to a good sex life.

This job didn't help my reputation with the more traditional locals. Rumors came back to me, as they do in small towns—the matriarch of the most respected farm family in town saying, "She has a different man every night at her house," another calling our remote neighborhood "the red-light district." At the time, three single women lived in isolated houses several miles apart and the snowplow driver, who was a family man, a fiddle player and our friend, used to stop by to visit. Any one of us would brew up cof-fee and chat away a good half hour on his timecard. I had my share of sexual friendships in those years and most of them, in memory, I treasure. But no lover ever became a coparent; I think I resisted that because so much was at stake for me in being a mother. I didn't trust anyone as much as I trusted myself. And I believed (though this is difficult now to own up to) that monogamy was about as noble an ideal as totalitarianism. I wanted to earn the respect of country people, and I thought I could do it by working hard for what I wanted and by being a good mother. But certain cultural borders seemed unbridgeable, and clearly the idea of sexual auton-omy as a morally responsible choice created one such boundary.

A few times during the decade I lived in the north, I worked in the woods. These jobs came as a great relief, usually after a fund-ing cut meant I'd been laid off from what had seemed a more per-manent job. The relief was not only economic, but a period of healing from the public tensions that women's health work increas-ingly entailed. I spent one spring near the end of that period work-ing the sugaring season at the zoologist's farm. Actually three couples had bought the place, but (typical of the fluidity of the times) only three of those six individuals remained. Two of them were former zoologists (one was the gull guy), now raising families and sheep, odd-jobbing, and taking a good portion of their annual income out of the trees.

We started on the first of March. At sunrise the temperature was still below zero—cold for March, even there. But layering up to work outdoors was a sign of spring, even if the robins were a long way off. The workhorses had grown woolly and cantankerous from a hard winter. Thornette and Joker were not a well-matched team. They had never worked together before, and Joker, a seventeen-year-old stocky black with a white blaze, had a bad reputation. He was wild, prone to prancing or bolting when what was needed was a steady pace. Thornette, a younger Belgian mare, preferred to nap on the job. We'd load the sleigh with firewood, then whip and whoop; she'd just stand there thigh-deep in crusty snow until we unloaded half of the burden. In harness together, Joker grew agitated, dancing and straining in the traces, while Thornette drooped in passive resistance. After several days of this, with the sun warming and the snow softening, the horses began to accept the inevitable: that they would have to work and that they would have to do so together—and they found a rhythm to match each other. Some early American farm machinery, reapers and combines, hitched sixteen or more horses together in harness. It's difficult to imagine how a contract was negotiated among so many equine personalities. But horses are herd animals, and so they are genetically prepared to work out their differences.

The sap didn't run until March 22, but we filled the weeks with hard days of labor—shimming the storage tank in the East Woods, gathering sled loads of firewood from the North Woods, adjusting and repairing the harnesses, drilling the tapholes (from one to eight taps per tree, depending on its girth), setting the spouts, and distributing thirty-five hundred lidded buckets throughout the woods. The ride was rough—stones, holes, and hummocks in the woods road or the natural tilt of the land pitching us off the sled and into the snow, stacks of buckets rolling down the hill. A bellyband or buckle, one of the traces or reins would break and someone would run back to the barn for the stuff to fix it, others heading indoors for coffee to wait out another delay. Conversation drifted from the weather, to gossip, to the owners' low-voiced hashing over of decisions—about a second mortgage, weighing the idea of setting up a land trust instead of private ownership, talk of a betrayal, arguments, the couple who'd left. For all the difficulties of their situation, they spoke with satisfaction of feeling closer to life than when they had studied it as scientists.

We waited and waited for the trees to loosen their juice. For sap to run sugar maples need warm sunny days and freezing nights. We had cold, cold, cold. Everything hip-deep in snow. We teamed out together into the sugarbush, the horses breaking roads through the snow. Then we fanned out separately to hang the buckets on the trees, sliding on lids to protect the sap from dirt, twigs, and rain, each one of us alone with thoughts and quiet. Then some slender music would drift up the hillside—birdcall, jangle of tugs, creak of sled-runners, rapping of stick against metal to separate the stacked buckets, birdsong of children arriving home from school. We found a porcupine den in a hollow tree in the Home Woods. Piss and shit by the entrance, twigs stripped bare and dropped out onto the snow, not a single pawprint farther than two feet from the tree, the creature's disgruntled assessment of the weather matching our own. Bird nests hung in the leafless trees like tangles in gray hair. Then we saw two robins, new orange against the black-and-white winter landscape (dark tree trunks against unmarred snow), and the mountains went pink in a bright sunset signaling a cold, clear night ahead and, we hoped, the necessary sunny day.

On the first day of gathering, the best tree in the bush had eight buckets all full, others had only an inch or two. We gathered the Home Woods, Heartbreak Hill, the Old Orchard, the names inherited from the family who had worked the sugarbush before us. Only a dozen people in the world know the names given to these clusters of trees, and they don't show up on any map, the names born from working, useful as tools. Trees are fifty years old before they are tapped; the best ones are two or three times that old. Someone who works the sugarbush for years gets to know how each tree runs, its relative productivity consistent over decades. The sap looks like clean water, tastes slightly sweet, and does not feel sticky. To make a gallon of maple syrup takes forty gallons of sap. We slogged through the snow each carrying two five-gallon pails, unhooked each bucket from the tree, poured the sap from bucket to pail, lugged pails from tree to tree until full, then to the steel tub on the sled, then teaming up to the next cluster of trees, and when the tub was full making a run to the gathering tank from which the sap would be piped downhill to the sugarhouse. We gathered nine tubs of sap and the first syrup came off Fancy, the highest grade, as light in color as clover honey.

Good sap runs come on only a handful of days each spring. By the time the trees bud, the sap is no good. If the day is too warm, the sap sours in the bucket. In the sugarhouse sap is boiled down on a wood-fired evaporator—the arch—which eats four-foot lengths of wood and sends billows of sweet steam out through the vented roof. On the good days we worked twelve backbreaking hours, gathering all morning, grading and canning the syrup into the night, and pasting on hand-lettered labels: HOME FARM: VERMONT MAPLE SYRUP. The rest of the time we waited, gathered firewood, and collected drizzle. In a season an average sugar maple gives ten gallons of sap, some give as much as eighty gallons. Having set thirty-five hundred taps, we did our share of slogging and lugging. Some days other neighbors and friends would come by to help for an hour or two, taking home a quart of syrup in trade. We had more visitors as the snow gave way to mud, the sled to a wagon, and we could finally start the day without long johns, the seasonal milepost that didn't come until April 18.

Spring takes its time in the north. Old-timers still talk about the year it never came, 1816, the year with no summer, when it snowed in July and one farmer reportedly saved his cornfield by cutting and burning pine trees around it day and night. This year spring came, though it was in no hurry. One week we saw the Canadian geese return from their winter migration, and the next a few green shoots began to pierce the leaf rot on the forest floor. The horses shed their winter coats in scrappy patches. A woodchuck ventured out of its hole, then baby rabbits, then the green began to leak up the hillsides as if slow capillary action were transforming meadow, then pasture, then foothill, then slope—the mountains holding their gray expressions until June. The last sap of the spring is called the frog run because it coincides with the first nightsongs of peepers. Its flavor is poor, bearing the woody bitterness of new buds. During cleanup at the end of April, restacking the buckets, pulling out the taps to let the drill holes heal, we found the first trout lilies in bloom, little yellow trumpets hanging amidst their fish-speckled leaves.

Now, reflecting back on that period, I find myself looking for possible meanings and for the reasons I left. I used to have a recurring dream there in which I lived in a dilapidated house, depressing in its demands for constant repair that I could not afford and did not have the skill to tackle alone. It was always winter in the dream; the furniture was spare and tattered; cold seeped through the seams around windows and doors; ice worked its way under the roofing, then melted and seeped around the chimney; the ceiling was marked with a spreading creosote stain. I dragged myself through room after room, exhausted, fearful that this house of entropy would collapse. I opened a door expecting to find more of the same and instead entered a luxurious library—the walls lined with bookshelves, hardbacks with gold-lettered spines stacked to the ceiling, a mahogany ladder on runners, deep oxblood-red leather chairs, Persian rugs, an oak desk on which a brass lamp sat glowing. Each time I dreamed this room, I experienced the same shock in finding it. How could it have been here in my house all along without my knowing it? Why did I live in ruin when I owned such riches?

Our time in the north was not an idyll. I found myself longing, on my own behalf and on Lucinda's, for the cultural dimension we'd left behind. We had to drive an hour and a half (often enough through snow and ice) to get to a movie, a concert, a decent library, or a fancy dessert. The alternative school went only to grade six and the parents who'd run it were too overworked to start another for the upper grades. The open classroom experience had given our kids exceptional social skills and creativity. In math and science, they were shaky. My daughter spent two years at the public middle school, where she was the only kid with brown bread in her lunch box. She took her share of grief for that and other evidence of her family's difference, but she still managed to be a gifted student. With all the talent sequestered in the hills, we found private teachers for piano, ballet, and riding lessons. But as high school approached, I grew leary of the patchwork nature of her education. Most local kids were raised to work on farms or join the army. Only two or three each year went to college; no one at the high school expected more. Luckily we were poor enough for her to receive scholarship offers from several private schools. I hoped that she'd choose an experimental one, but she said, "No more hippie schools, Mom," and we packed her off to a traditional bastion of the New England elite.

For myself, though I never stopped imagining that I could be a full-time farmer, working the land was either a hobby or a stopgap job. My public health career burned out the year that federal money for sexually transmitted diseases (a hush-hush budget item even fifteen years ago) was diverted into the high-profile campaign to fight a nonexistent swine flu epidemic. I ended the seventies in an unhappy relationship, made the mistake of thinking a material solution would solve emotional problems, and sold my farm to buy one with my live-in love. We struggled for a few years to make that arrangement work. In my imaginative life, intimate relationship is central: I am constantly falling in love and living out the years in dynamic connection with a loved one. Yet by midlife a theme emerges from one's experience, which may be at odds with what one has imagined. I'm surprised to see how peripheral intimate relationships have been for me, coming and going like jobs, addresses, and seasons. What sense of continuity and connectedness I've known has come from being a mother, a writer, a gardener, and from friendship. I suppose my old neighbors would continue to find my experience either shocking or sad. I moved away from farm country to a small city that offered a good bakery, several bookstores, an ocean view, a university, walkable streets, and neighbors I did not know. It was a dark time. I was weighed down with grief for what I'd left. In a journal I wrote this entry: "*Skototropism,* meaning to grow toward darkness; a behavioral trait of vines in the tropical forest that enables them to find trees to climb. They head across the forest floor to the darkest spot, sun-shielded and wet, all their energy focused, an arrow pointed toward survival."

THREE

THE CHACO
PHENOMENON

I'VE HAD TO WORK SINCE I WAS NINETEEN, RAISING A
daughter alone. That necessity and my personal need to do work
that matters in some way other than the gleaning of a paycheck has
meant I've been unable to know the pleasure of staying in one
place. In August 1990, I found myself heading for the Sonoran
Desert. My A.C.–free Toyota had a thermostat set for New
England, giving me two choices for refreshment: fan on for a sweet
jet of engine heat in the face, or fan off for window blasts of
asphalt-enhanced desert scorch. It's a dry heat, the Southwest
enthusiasts boast, as if a 110-degree day could be rendered comfortable by that arid claim. I felt the moisture burning out of my
skin, my eyes stinging with dryness, an overheated exhaustion
overcoming my eagerness to get where I was going. After six days
of headlong highway prayer—the steel about to pop through my
thinning radial tires, car cantilevering across the barren flatlands,
then the panhandle nightmare of stockyards steaming with the last
rank heat of cattle penned for slaughter, the overland pipes and
blinking grid where oil fields meet the refinery—I fell blessedly into
a haven of clean sheets, room service, and machine-made cold air.

My last night before hitting Arizona I spent in a gaudy motel in
Deming, New Mexico. It seemed only fitting, though I know of no
literal or genetic connection between myself and those who named
that billboarded, sweltering town. Being in Deming, it seemed,
would let me pretend that I was comfortably at home. I was mov-

ing from Provincetown—a town with a constantly reconfiguring yet nourishing community of artists and writers, a town where I knew how and when and where to catch a bluefish or a bucket of squid or to pick a quart of wild cranberries—to Tucson, where I didn't know a soul except the members of the search committee who had offered me a job. I guess that's how most of us move these days, for some practical reason, rather than because we're in love with a place.

The last stretch of road I had traveled was Route 26, the hypotenuse of the triangle formed by Deming, Hatch, and Las Cruces. Taking that shortcut means driving through fifty miles of nothing on a two-lane road—one bend, if memory serves me, with a closed gas station and an open redneck bar. Nothing for company on the shoulderless span but barrel-assing semis and creeping farm machinery, though what crop could be cultivated there I couldn't imagine. The blank expanse of land looked stark, ugly, and hostile. I longed for lushness, for unexpected clouds, for the dense and nestling woods of my Northeast home ground—land that had given shape to my imagination.

Driving through nature usually makes me write, as if an emanation comes from the land, inducing language as an aroma induces hunger. "Breathe in experience, breathe out poetry," wrote Muriel Rukeyser, locating the habit smack-dab in the midst of our biology. I think she was right to do so. This writing response in me is as automatic as sneezing in a field of tassled grass. Perhaps there's a small burl on one of my chromosomes that causes the verbal propensity. Is it adaptive or merely an incidental tick, like the tendency of my left foot to grow a bunion? I understand the genetic advantage of feeling joyful when one comes upon an expanse of pure, clear water or a verdant stand of cottonwoods and grasses. The land mammal who favors such scenery has a higher likelihood of survival than one who is drawn to gravel and slime. But I'm not sure whether the compulsion to write is a genetic advantage or disadvantage. Human language has been used so often to control, oppress, and misunderstand others, rather than to nurture and preserve.

Alastair Reid in "Looking for Hispaniola" gives a moving account of Columbus renaming the capes, headlands, bays, points, and rivers of that newfound land. No matter that the Taino Indians already had names and stories for all those places. The first act of cultural erasure in the so-called new world was an act of language, and it opened the invader's mind to uncountable horrors to come—the erasing of people, their music, their history, and the sense that they belonged to the land. All life forms are entrepreneurial, harboring the ability to establish a niche in the most inhospitable places, to displace their competition, to grow fat on the weakness and misfortune of others. Taking over new territory is a survival mechanism—one of the skills the land has inspired in order to perpetuate its own evolutionary improvisations. So too must be the ongoing process of naming. One takes the new place in through the senses and asks the land to reciprocate by offering new words. The process of naming has an evolution as well, inspiring a sense of renewal, of reaching to correct the inaccuracies of the past, of retelling the stories we live by so that they sustain rather than shame us.

That summer when I first drove through the sizzling desert scrub, I felt not the joy and vocabulary of the new place so much as its challenge and silence. The sky was dazzling, grand, expansive. Yet everything that thrived beneath it had spines and venom. The fantasy of subsisting off the land—the true American dream and one of the ways I make myself at home in a place—seemed unthinkable. Living on lizard, rattlesnake, creosote bush, and yucca root did not look nearly as attractive as the pleasures of deer, wild mushrooms, acorns, and blackberries. And there was the question of water, always the serious question of water. I tried to picture the ancient people who had populated the desert for thousands of years before the incursion of the Europeans, tribes whose vibrant afterimage can still be read in the landscape and communities of the Southwest. How had those people survived so long in a place so violently hot and arid? In August, what little vegetation the land had managed to eke out looked dead or dying. No shelter in sight. Streambeds were dried gouges of grainy sand and crumbled limestone—not a particle of nourishing peat or silt. I stopped to piss in the roadside scrub and couldn't stop my nervous scanning of the ground, anticipating rattlers, scorpions, and tarantulas crawling out of every tuft of desiccated grass. It seemed too much to ask of one's attention to watch out for these vermin and still hope to see this place. The midday radiation bit into me like lasers. I slapped on sunscreen, gulped warm water from the canteen, and began to feel my good English metaphors—"Shall I compare thee to a summer's day?"—fall away, along with my gardening skills, my ability to read the sky and the seasons, and my confidence that moving to Tucson was a good idea. Nature might be, as John Haines has written, "the great book we have been reading, and writing, from the beginning." But this chapter I might have to skip.

AFTER TWENTY-SIX MILES OF INSUFFERABLE DIRT WASHBOARD through the high desert of the Navajo nation, I snake through the boulder-lined pass down into Chaco Canyon, a ragged gouge cut by the wash that spills south—when it runs—from the San Juan River. I have lived in the Southwest for three years and I haven't given up trying to read its text. 5 P.M.—the visitor center locked, a gray-haired ranger pulleying down the flag for the night. "Oh sure," he tells me, "go on ahead. There are plenty of campsites." And for once it's true. A modest campground—no drinking water, no snack bar, no phone. Just two or three small loops for trailers and one for walk-in campers, the whole cluster tucked along the base of a weather-worn limestone cliff. I pitch my tent in the back end of a box canyon, the site fairly private, offering a sandy tent pad, picnic table, and a fire pit ringed with a hunk of corrugated culvert. Campsite number twelve. Above, graceful lacework worn in the limestone—a network of melon-sized concavities where water has slowly swished away the rock. Cliff swallows work the evening air, bringing insects back to the mudnests plastered under the overhangs. The swallows' colony of cliff dwellings looks exactly as the Peterson's guide describes—"gourdlike jugs of mud." Each time a bird swoops up with a delivery, the excited peeping of chicks echoes out of the clay drums. The rounded forms of the nests seem to echo the rounded hollows washed into the rock. Maybe seeing those hollows gave the birds the idea of building such structures. How *did* the swallows figure out their masonry technique? By accident, I suppose. After centuries of picking up straw, sticks, and seed fluff for nesting materials, some geeky forebear of these evening fliers grabbed a few hunks of muddy grass and its nest began to harden into something more secure than a pile of weeds. Still, the distance seems great, the learning minutely incremental, from that small act to this pueblo of smoothly sculpted mudnests.

I've packed in firewood, since the park allows no wood gathering. I have yet to succumb to buying a camp stove, though I would relish the convenience I am sure. Yet to trade the sweet scent and whispering of a campfire for the hiss and efficiency of a gas-burning stove is not my cup of tea. I prefer the hardware-store coffee pot perched teetering at the fire's edge. I love the labor and patience of a woodfire, the uncertainty as the kindling catches or fails to—rebuilding the air-fed structure of graduated twigs, sticks, and logs when the catching doesn't go right. I usually follow the tepee method, leaning the sticks together to form a cone until the flame is established. Sometimes I use the log cabin method, laying two sticks flat, then two more on top at right angles, and so forth until I've built a Lincoln log house to set on fire. As darkness begins to close around the camp, black space starts opening, the stars winking forth one at a time. No matter where or when people on earth have lived—under palms, baobabs, sugar maples, or arctic sky—they've known the same moon, the same sheen of blackness flecked with white, the same shooting whispers of light that, even as they disappear, make us draw in our breath and exclaim. No matter the differences in what we believe we are seeing, the experience of scale and wonder must be, at heart, the same. The questions of the night, the same. Who are we? How did we come to be this wondering inward animal in a universe of stony silences? Why are we here? Where are we going?

As I wait for those minutes of transformation, the sky dims to gray—no sign yet of Jupiter or the evening stars. A bat loops up close to the overhang where the nestlings lie in their mud jugs. Dusk is deepening. The swallows appear to have tucked in for the night, but a few rouse themselves to warn off the bat. Again and again the furred flier swirls in manic approach and retreat. The swallows respond, defending their airspace, though they can't match the intense, jagged speed of the interloper. Darker now—the swallows quiet into sleep leaving the bat to its business. On the clifftop, overlooking the bat-and-swallow show, sits another bird—somewhat bigger than the swallows, plump and long tailed, perhaps a sparrow hawk. It alternately preens and watches until full dark, when it slips behind the backside of the ridge. The night amplifies small sounds—or perhaps the sense of hearing becomes more finely tuned as there is less to see. Sounds drift by like thin smoke—the indistinct voices of other campers, the clink of cookware, hiss of stoves, zipping of tents, thunking of car trunks, a throat clearing, the modulating flame of the campfire blowing its gentle riff.

CHETRO KETL. PUEBLO BONITO. KIN KLETSO. CASA RINCONADA. Tsin Kletsin. Una Vida. Pueblo Alto. Peñasco Blanco. The names of the ruins came from the Navajo people, who settled here several hundred years after the master builders of the Anasazi had abandoned Chaco Canyon. Or perhaps, to state this more accurately, these names came from the Spanish version of the Navajo names.

This place bears the imprint of successive misunderstandings—Anasazi to Navajo, Navajo to Spanish, Spanish to American. The Anasazi had no written language, but aspects of their history can be read in the artifacts of their cities and in the land to which they adapted over thousands of years. Much has been lost, much pillaged. Even the word by which we call them to mind expresses loss—*Anasazi,* from the Navajo, meaning *ancient strangers.* Even the ruins will fall to ruin, though that process has been slowed by their protection as a national historical park. Some of the great masonry walls, which climb four stories high, are braced with struts and steel plates. Much of my method in trying to know the ancient strangers—going out to look around, then reading up on the accumulated research and watching documentary films—stems from a tradition entirely uncharacteristic of their ways. Whatever language I find to describe and understand the Anasazi will never be their language. This quality of mystery about their lives is what draws my curiosity so profoundly. How did they describe the mudnests of the cliff swallows? The black silk canopy of night sky? The places on the bank of the San Juan River where they gathered clay? With what words did they ask for what they lacked? What did the strands of shell and turquoise (some up to seventeen feet long) found in sealed niches in the great kiva at Chetro Ketl mean to their women, to their men? What words did they speak in fear, or in love; what prayers were whispered or sung when the dead were curled, knees to chest, an arc of black-on-white pots arranged over the head? Those strains of the planet's music are gone for good.

I AM OUT EARLY TOURING THE SITES. THERE ARE NO CROWDS AND I'm thankful. The mind needs space to comprehend certain things. Having nothing but space on these arid mesas and canyonlands, the Anasazi built immense cellular structures of squared-off stone. Pueblo Bonito is the largest and most thoroughly excavated.

Shaped like a massive D, it grew to more than six hundred multi-leveled contiguous rooms, forty underground kivas, and two great plazas. By cellular, I mean the way a stained membrane of an onion looks under a microscope—each tiny unit annexed by another and another, each walled off, yet connected, forming a gracefully integrated whole. On wall after wall, shaped stone meets shaped stone with precision, walls climbing into perfect vertical planes, the planes arcing to form the pueblo's semicircular perimeter, square rooms, and round kivas. Both in small detail and in overall architectural design, the physical properties of the structure—even in its present state of partial ruin—are masterful, orderly, and beautiful.

Pueblo Bonito, according to tree-ring data gathered from structural timbers, was built and occupied from the 900s to about 1200—the period of the Chaco Anasazi's cultural flowering. It was built by people who did not have the use of metal, writing, or mathematics—as we know them. Whatever tools and language they did use were clearly adequate for the task. Whatever means they used to enhance their memories, learn from experience, and visualize complex architectural projects, clearly adequate for the task. The masonry technique, refined from the simple slab structures of their ancestors, employed large blocks of irregular sandstone that were chinked with smaller stones and set into mud mortar. Where structures needed greater strength and stability, the builders used a core-and-veneer style of masonry—orderly exterior courses of shaped stone built up around an inner core of rubble. As lovely as the stonework is, there is evidence that the walls were covered with mud plaster. Rooms in the pueblo are not separated by hallways. Rather, rooms open one into the other through low doorways. Room after room after room lined up and stacked up—like hundreds of empty boxes in a warehouse.

Archaeologists agree that it is unclear what the rooms were used for. Probably some were for living and some were for storage. At one time, researchers thought that each room was a dwelling—making population estimates for the area much higher than is currently believed. Debris layered in the dirt at Pueblo Bonito suggests patterns of use and nonuse. Now the experts think that by A.D. 1000 there were between two thousand and five thousand people living in several hundred small to medium villages and a dozen large towns around the Chaco Plateau—perhaps as many as a thousand people at one time living in Pueblo Bonito. This large pueblo is thought to have been a central depot for production and distribution of crops, as well as for trade with peoples from the south. Imported seashells, copper bells, feathers of parrots and macaws have been found at the site. The Anasazi grew crops on the canyon's arid land by channeling rainwater off the cliffs or from side canyons and gullies. They built terraces, dams, stone-lined canals, and ditches. But there probably never was enough water here to comfortably support the crops they needed. Trade, interdependence with outlying groups, was essential to their flower-ing. More than four hundred miles of prepared footroads, some up to thirty feet wide, connect Chaco to dozens of communities in the San Juan River Basin, with settlements located at one-day travel intervals stretching into what is now Utah, Colorado, and Arizona. Sections of roadway are lined with stone walls or rows of large boulders. The ground had been leveled, roads plotted to run straight for miles, no matter how rough the original terrain. Long-distance communication outposts were perched on mesa tops and cliffs from which a signal fire could be read in distant villages. At Pueblo Alto, a ruin on the mesa just above Pueblo Bonito, archae-ologists found huge quantities of animal bones and imported potsherds. Again the debris was layered, indicating periods of use and nonuse. The evidence suggests, according to Park Service literature, that the site "was not so much lived in as used periodi-cally by large groups of Anasazi for ceremonies, which included feasting and ritual breaking of pottery (both of which are known in pueblo societies)." Pueblo Bonito, as well, was likely a center for sacred ritual, with crowds gathering from outlying towns for brief

community experiences, then leaving the site to the care of custodians, priests, and bureaucrats.

What all of this adds up to is "the Chaco phenomenon"—a
rapid technological ascent and decline of a culture that had lived
for ten thousand years in the American Southwest. The early people had stalked bison and mammoth. They began an agricultural
life around A.D. 400, settling into shallow pit houses lined with a
single course of flat stone, covered with brush and mud. Perhaps
they learned mud masonry from watching the cliff swallows. They
harvested corn, squash, and beans—originally wild foods that had
migrated north from Mexico—and gathered dozens of indigenous
plants for food, tools, clothing, and shelter. Juniper and grease-
wood were used for firewood, cliffrose bark for baskets, rope, and
sandals. They ate the seeds of the four-wing saltbush, used its
leaves and twigs for yellow dye. They slept on woven willow mats
and often were buried in them. Around A.D. 800 they began to
develop masonry techniques and construct arcing rows of single-
story storage rooms with the pit houses clustered in the center of
the arc. Later these outer storage rooms were converted into living
and working spaces, but the older central pit structures such as the
ceremonial kiva remained a part even of the great houses, Pueblo
Bonito and Pueblo del Arroyo.

By 1300, Chaco Canyon had been abandoned, its culture disin-
tegrated under the pressure of a prolonged drought that afflicted
the Southwest for nearly a hundred years. As the local resources
dwindled, most people shifted to the south and southeast—
regrouping on what have become the Hopi and Zuni lands.
Perhaps their descendants also included the people of the Acoma
and Laguna Pueblos of northern New Mexico. There is no historical record of the Anasazi's lineage, no clear line of cultural inheritance of the Chaco people's engineering, architectural, artistic,
and organizational prowess. In the 1500s Navajos migrated into
Chaco Canyon, where they lived and grazed sheep through several
centuries of war and peace, Spanish and Anglo exploration,

"intrigue, violence, litigation, rustling and murder," until finally the last Navajo family living in the canyon was relocated in 1948.

The ruins are a partial text written in a language we can't read. Archaeologists keep working to fill in the blanks. What can be inferred about the people who lived here? Unlike in our society, the unit of organization was the clan or band, not the individual or the family. The cellular style of architecture testifies to this—the lack of private quarters of a size suitable for separate families. Their sense of community must have been much more immediate than ours. Like us, they had a propensity and talent for technology and organization. They played out these talents with far fewer technical aids, suggesting that their minds were more orderly and patient than ours. Tribal people who still have a working knowledge of an oral tradition speak of sharing a collective responsibility for cultural memory. Certain areas are assigned to certain individuals, and the elders make the young people practice until they get the telling right. Like us, the Chaco Anasazi had a developed ability to give form to their ideas and pass them on. They knew an intimacy with the land that we, for all of our scientific knowledge, will never know. Their subsistence was tightly woven with the environment, the fluctuations of the seasons, the dry and wet days and years. Even in incidental ways their relationship with place was more intimate than ours. Driving through nature with bugs splattering on the windshield is clearly a more remote point of view than walking through desert saltbush, crickets jumping onto bare calves.

Like us, the ancient Americans studied the vastness and detail of the night sky. A pictograph on the trail to Peñasco Blanco depicts the supernova explosion recorded by Chinese and Japanese astronomers in 1054. Painted red and yellow in a shallow overhang is a spiral, above it a sunburst, crescent moon, and a human hand—the latter suggesting that the site was sacred. On July 4, 1054, the crescent moon came within two degrees of the supernova that produced what we call the Crab Nebula. The Asian astronomers recorded that a bright star shone so brightly it could be seen in daylight for two weeks. Contemporary astrophysicist Rudolf Kippenhahn writes that "in 1054 Ibn Butlan, a doctor in Constantinople, held a celestial phenomenon responsible for an epidemic in which about fifteen hundred people died. The site of this strange manifestation was at the approximate site of the Crab supernova explosion." We don't know what meaning that sky event had for the people of Chaco Canyon—but that it had meaning we can be sure. Like us, they knew an epiphany when they saw one and they recorded it in the most permanent medium available to them. Like us, they loved beauty. Their pottery is more than functional. Its painted geometric designs—jagged or coiled black lines on white clay—are complex and harmonious. The forms are graceful—elegant roundness, tapering or flared necks—pinched and pressed together from coils of clay without the help of a potter's wheel.

We find it mysterious that these people "disappeared." But they didn't. They starved, died of thirst and disease, and of necessity walked away from their beautiful cities, from the tradition that gave them both a past and a future—the chain of influences we call a culture, which gives people a sense of who they are and how they ought to live their lives. I remember hearing Eliza Jones, an Athabaskan storyteller and linguist from northern Alaska, speak about the disruptive post-European influences in her people's lives. She said that the most damaging thing had been education—native children sent to "Indian schools" in Oregon and Arizona. In traditional village life, all of the adults took responsibility for the children in the area and education happened through storytelling. She was a member of the last generation to be raised in this way. In the evenings the children would lie on the floor listening to the stories of elders; they would grow sleepy and spread out their bedrolls in the one-room house, the stories continuing to stream into their minds, awake or asleep. When they were old enough to start telling stories themselves, they were strictly supervised and trained. Traditional stories offered lessons, looking to the community's past for guidance into the future. Children taken by missionary Whites from the northern villages were combined with other tribal people from unrelated communities. They learned neither the traditional ways of their own people, nor how to survive in the White world. They fit in nowhere. The Anasazi culture, in contrast, was disrupted by the natural forces of drought and overworking of the land. But as the Anasazi drifted away from their homelands, from their traditions and accomplishments, they must have suffered a similar kind of disorienting grief.

When my blood ancestors wrenched themselves from England in the 1600s, they came to America to be free of history. They left a densely settled checkerboard of cities, towns, and pastures for (as they saw it) a howling wilderness from which they needed God's protection, in which they intended to sow the seeds of God's new garden. But when they entered that new relationship with nature, they didn't leave history—they entered it as a culturally dispossessed people without a homeland. This continent to them was a symbolic place—they knew nothing about its plants and weather, even less about its people and their history—that long wisdom inspired by the land.

What was happening among my ancestors, the European fibers of which I'm woven, during Chaco's heyday and the period of its dissolution—the years, roughly speaking, between 1000 and 1300? No one knew that the American continent existed. There had been no Chaucer. No Shakespeare. Land was owned by the rich and farmed hierarchically—vassals managed fiefdoms, work was done by serfs. A manor house lorded over each community—around it the thatched huts of peasants and land cultivated with wooden plows and sticks. Serfs kept a few chickens and geese, but were not allowed to hunt, as the nobles did for sport. One gets the sense that Europe was already crowded—two hundred thousand people living in Paris alone in the twelfth century. The cornerstones were laid for Westminster Abbey and the Cathedral of Notre-Dame, great Gothic celebrations of an authoritarian God. Monasteries were the enclaves of learning and writing; sacred texts were lettered by elegant hand and dressed in jewels and gold, while outside the holy walls peasants and townsfolk hungered, the land overused, drained, and eroded. In Coventry, England, the first feminist activist, Lady Godiva, rode naked through town on a white horse after her husband, the local earl, promised to repeal a burdensome tax on the citizenry if she would do so. The Crusades began—a failed series of religious wars against the Moslems that lasted 200 years. Soldiers, both nobles and peasants, left Europe in droves for Constantinople. Those who returned brought with them the Black Death, which would kill nearly three quarters of the population of Europe and Asia—and, ironically, would help to restore ecological balance between human population and natural resources.

If I could be sent by time machine back to the year 1100 and if I could pick my own tribe, I'd cast my lot with the Chaco Anasazi. I'd rather learn what they knew about patience, collective living, and intimacy with the land than the hierarchical, acquisitive, warmongering ways of my forebears. The very word we use to describe the European social system of that period—feudal—says that their lives were based on conflict and contention. And yet, *I am* that tradition. I write. I acquire new ideas and insights and place them hierarchically above the old ones. I am obsessed with this process of "making it new" through language, of improving my relationships with people and places by removing myself to the solitude of my desk. This is a gift from my ancestry that I treasure. So I would not climb on board the time machine unless I could bring with me paper and pens. And I don't mean to be romantically primitivistic about the ancient Americans. I know they practiced war, brutality, and ritual human sacrifice, that they suffered disease and injustice. A Pawnee recently told me that his people sacrificed a young virgin (usually a woman, sometimes a man) to Mother Corn every year well into the 1800s, until some heretic finally questioned whether the corn harvest really depended on such a death. But the undercurrent of American Indian lives sprang from *this* land

and they drank deeply, believing that a diffused spirituality was present in all things including their own bodies. Their degree of engagement—physical and spiritual—with nature was medicine my ancestors needed, never got.

"How did they do it?" the tourists ask in astonishment, surveying the ruin of Pueblo del Arroyo. It is the question we ask when we see photographs taken from the moon, the Cathedral of Notre-Dame, the calendric structures of Stonehenge, or the sky city of Machu Picchu. We have a reverence for all pasts, in part it seems because we can't quite believe our own technological abilities as a species. Pueblo del Arroyo was the last great house to be built in the canyon. It contained two hundred eighty rooms and more than twenty kivas, was built over a relatively short period of time— maybe twenty-five years—and was as shaped by belief as the Gothic cathedrals. How could "prehistoric" people construct such stunning things? How cut the stones flat? How find, cut, and haul a tree twenty-six inches in diameter and set it for a roof pillar? How visualize the placement of each stone to form the perfect cylinder of a ceremonial kiva twelve feet deep with its encircling stone bench, its niches, vaults, underground entranceways, and its celestial alignment? The leap from the stone-slab pit house to Pueblo Bonito is as significant as the leap from the combustion engine to walking on the moon. We are a global culture now, sharing a common future and a common past—periods of flowering and decay. Everyone inherits everyone else's legacy; everyone is claimed by the land.

As I DRIVE BACK UP THROUGH THE BOULDERED PASS LEAVING THE canyon, wild sagebrush sprawls as far as I can see on the surrounding plateau, a pungent low-lying haze of dusty green that thrives on the arid sun-bleached land. Miles of dirt road cut through the high chaparral—Navajo hogans posted with slapdash signs for religious revivals. It's no surprise to me that the Navajo consider sage to be sacred and use it in ritual ceremonies. It fills the stark plateau with lushness, volatility, and evergreen persistence. The scent in my car after I pick a bunch makes my eyes water for hundreds of miles.

From a low-flying plane one could see on this bleached and open terrain the green lines marking the grasses and locoweed that have grown on the prepared soil where once the Anasazi roadbeds lay. Like a giant game of connect the dots, the lines take form and converge. The land looks different from the ground too—each mound in the talus, each weedy rise in the short-grass prairie, every dark green smear along a canyon or wash becoming the possibility of a village where broken vessels and tangled dreams lie, where the spirit of a beautiful handmade city hovers, the land growing more verdant where those others have walked before.

 # THE PETRIFIED FOREST

1934. BLACK MESA, ARIZONA.

A gas station and cafe at a lonely crossroads in the desert—one way leading to Phoenix, another to the Petrified Forest. Autumn. Boulders and dirt road purpling in the sunset. The Black Mesa Bar-B-Q is a family business. Gramps, a wizened celebrant of the Wild West, who still thinks a gangster is the true American hero. Jason, the dull and paunchy legionnaire, a World War veteran who loves to wear a uniform and feel necessary. And Gabrielle, Jason's daughter by a war marriage to a French woman who has long since fled the desert, leaving her spirited offspring with a copy of François Villon, a dream of art and freedom, and a dead-end job that nominally, at least, reduces her from angel-of-comfort to the distinctly more trivial "Gabby"—played by an effervescent Bette Davis. In poems Gabby finds solace—"They get the stink of the gasoline and the hamburger out of my system." Enter, Alan Squier—dressed in tweed jacket, flannel trousers, and felt hat—approaching on foot with a walking stick and a rucksack in which he carries a copy of Jung's *Modern Man in Search of a Soul* and an insurance policy. He bears "the afterglow of elegance," in the words of playwright Robert Sherwood, a hue conveyed by Leslie Howard with a beautifully sad charm. Squier, a failed writer, belongs to "a vanishing race ... the intellectuals."

"That means you've got brains," says Gabby.

"Yes—brains without purpose," he replies. "Noise without sound. Shape without substance. Have you ever read 'The Hollow

Men?' Don't. It's discouraging, because it's true. It refers to the intellectuals, who thought they'd conquered nature. They dammed it up and used its waters to irrigate the wastelands. They built streamlined monstrosities to penetrate its resistance. They wrapped it up in cellophane and sold it to drugstores. They were so certain they had it subdued. And now—do you realize what it is that is causing world chaos? ... It's nature hitting back. Not with the old weapons—floods, plagues, holocausts. We can neutralize them. She's fighting back with strange instruments called neuroses. She's deliberately afflicting mankind with the jitters. Nature is proving that she can't be beaten—not by the likes of us. She's taking the world away from the intellectuals and giving it back to the apes."

"You know, you talk like a goddam fool," Gabby tells him, but the love charm of a man on the road, embarked on the great American soul quest, has done its work on her. She wants to go with him to Paris to live in sin, learn about art and cathedrals, and "have one hell of a time."

Headed this way—to complete the triumvirate of head, heart, and brawn—is Duke Mantee, the world-famous killer, his gang on the run from a shoot-out in Oklahoma City, where they've killed six, wounded four, two of the wounded not expected to live. Mantee, like Squier, is a man the world left behind—both of them condemned to outmoded lives—though Bogie's saturnine portrayal of the gangster gives the Wild West a taste of Chicago-style, big-business crime.

"Certainly it's revolution ..." are the first words in the script, spoken by a workman stopped for lunch, talking with his buddy about what's needed in this country before we'll have equality. So far democracy has meant, "Everyman for himself! That's the kind of liberty we've been getting." He admires the Russian Revolution for pioneering a vision "for the benefit of all."

"They don't have crime in Russia," he boasts, "because they've abolished the cause of crime. They've abolished greed!" 1934. The United States newly awakened from postwar complacency by the

Great Depression, the dust bowl. The tumbleweed-blown cafe plastered with tin signs—Apache Beer, Gas and Oil, N.R.A., American Legion—not exactly a haven for a red-thinking worker.

Mantee and his gang show up, taking everyone hostage—including a rich couple in a Dusenberg driven by their Black chauffeur, who conveniently happen to pass through on their way to Santa Monica, giving further dimension to the theme of democracy's failure—and Squier takes inspiration from the mineralized trees up the road. The male fossils square off.

Squier, with a taunting half-smile: "I'm planning to be buried in the Petrified Forest. I've been evolving a theory about that that would interest you. It's the graveyard of the civilization that's been shot out from under us. It's the world of outmoded ideas. Platonism—Patriotism—Christianity—Romance—the Economics of Adam Smith—they're all so many dead stumps in the desert. That's where I belong—and so do you, Duke. For you're the last great apostle of rugged individualism. Aren't you?"

"Maybe you're right, pal."

"I'm eternally right. But what use do I make of it?"

To be of use, finally, is Squier's all-American quest and he hatches a plan. He signs his life insurance policy over to Gabby— the love charm of a woman whose vitality has not been tainted by the world, for whom Europe is a romance not a battleground, has done its work on him. Yet so passionless a man is he that his great act of love is to have Mantee shoot him so that he can leave five thousand corporate dollars to Gabrielle and her dreams.

"In killing me, you'd only be executing the sentence of the law— I mean, natural law, survival of the fittest. Living, I'm worth nothing to her. Dead, I can buy her the tallest cathedrals and golden vineyards and dancing in the streets.... Don't you see? ... She's the future. She's the renewal of vitality—and courage—and aspiration—all the strength that has gone out of you. Hell—I can't say what she is—but she's essential to me, and the whole damned country, and the whole miserable world."

Squier's suicidal deal is a strange act of heroism, expressing both self-sacrifice and ultimate self-interest. He has found his purpose in falling in love, yet can't imagine sticking around to express his love as ongoing care. To become a man of action, rather than one of unactualized ideals, he gets himself taken permanently out of action. But the marriage between the old world and the new that he arranges for Gabby is another unactualized ideal. She becomes, in his eyes, not a woman he might love, but a symbol of virginal "natural" America, which cannot thrive without returning to its roots in the high art and poetry of Europe. Squier's rhetoric about leaving the world of outmoded ideas proves as empty, in his last act, as his view of the western landscape. He can't escape his nature or his fate any more than can Mantee. By the time the big shoot-out comes, Squier's already so removed that he feels like he's "on a penguin island watching these strange creatures run about." And Gabrielle has returned to her book.

1993. THE PETRIFIED FOREST NATIONAL PARK. BADLANDS.
Soft mudstone eroding in chalky streams, rivelled humps and mesas melting away. Bare stratified layers—gray, white, tan, rose. Centuries of particles and rot building up, washing and blowing away. Sandstone, siltstone, clay. A tuft or two of grass, needle-thin yucca, spindly Mormon tea. Collapsed blocky segments—crude cylinders—where gigantic trees turned to stone have tumbled out of the crumbling dirt. Puffs of cloud forming a high plateau, defining an aerial plane that goes on for fifty miles. The clouds gray on the bottom, sunlight radiating off the billowing tops, the upper edges highlighted in gold. Above—blue sky—a map of the sea with broad, clustering islands of cloud.

The place is the afterlife of a tropical forest that grew here during the age of the dinosaurs, when this continent was several thousand miles southeast of its present location. Arizona was at the latitude of Panama, this now desiccated land covered with humid swamps and marshes, dense vegetation—tree ferns, horsetail, and palmlike cycads. Rivers and streams running through the region carried sediment from the volcanic highlands of the Mogollon rim—sand and silt and clay that settled out as the waters slowed crossing the flat plateau. Timbers fallen in the highlands washed down and settled into the mud. Fish, clams, amphibians, crayfish, beetles, and locusts thrived. Flying reptiles—pterosaurs and icarosaurs— droned the birdless air, fought, died, and decayed in the seeping muck. Layer upon layer of organic matter was covered by heavy wet sediment, compressed into what geologists now call the Chinle Formation.

Petrification occurs when the cells in decaying organisms are replaced by minerals. As the organic matter leaches out, crystals form in the spaces between the tissues. A petrified fossil keeps the shape of the life form—down to bark, knot holes, and even the original cell walls—but its meat becomes stone. Among the trees buried in the Chinle Formation are massive conifers— *Araucarioxylon arizonicum*—that grew nearly as large as redwoods, some up to two hundred feet tall and ten feet across. Members of their family still grow in warm, humid parts of Australia, New Zealand, and South America. These giants became the fractured blocks that lie in domino strands along the desert. What if prevailing conditions on the planet had been such that all ancient decaying organic matter had become fossilized as rock, rather than pressure-treated to become coal and oil? What would our species have made of itself then? The fact that some fossils turned to gasoline and some to quartz is a fluke of nature, a product of complex circumstance and changing weather. The process of petrification isn't fully understood—what exact constellation of variables makes it occur. Acidic swamp water laden with silicon particles probably covered the fallen logs, seeping through the wood and slowing its decay. The silicon combined with oxygen in the wood and formed tiny crystals of quartz (silicon dioxide), and where the logs contained hollows the growth of crystals ran wild—

rose quartz, smoky quartz, and amethysts. Other elements carried in the water stained the growing rock with zones of cobalt blue, iron reds and yellows, seeping veins of black manganese and carbon. Sometime after they had fallen and hardened, the trees cracked into fractured logs during earthquakes—many of them sectioned off neatly like lumber that's been felled, bucked up into two-foot lengths, and lies waiting for the splitter.

The Petrified Forest is the afterlife of a species, and it is tempting here to imagine the afterlife of ours—as if our passing could ever be so clean. What we will leave behind will look less like art and more like a monumental, mindless dump. The memory of organic process will have been perfected in these petrified trees that gave themselves over, cell by cell, to recording the history of their passing.

1906. ORAIBI, ARIZONA.
Earle Forrest, growing up in Pennsylvania, read about the snake dance of the Hopis and wondered whether the stories could be true. He came west to Flagstaff and rode for the Babbitt Brothers C-O-Bar Ranch, covering rangeland from Montana to Mexico. It took him four years to wend his way to Oraibi, where he witnessed the snake dance ritual and wrote down what he saw. Nine days before the ceremony the members of the Snake and Antelope Societies went to their kivas to prepare. They spent four days gathering hundreds of snakes—big desert diamondbacks, smaller prairie rattlers, sidewinders, bull snakes, whip snakes, garter snakes. The majority were rattlers, caught under protection of prayer. The snakes were taken to the kiva, guarded, and washed in a large bowl containing six gourdsful of prepared water. Some accounts say the water contained cornmeal, others that it was mixed with a yellow herb—golindrina or yerba. The snakes were thrown into clean sand, herded by boys with snake whips—eagle feathers tied to a wooden handle. If a snake began to coil, a boy

waved his feather whip along its spine and the snake would uncurl, wanting only to escape, because "the eagle is the enemy of the snake and will suddenly swoop down."

Earle Forrest reports that two thousand Indians and fifty Whites gathered in the plaza on the day of the dancing, the roofs of the stone houses covered with Indians. Edward Curtis was there with a movie camera, allegedly having paid the Snake Society two hundred dollars for the privilege of filming in the Snake kiva. As the sun began to sink behind the San Francisco peaks, an Indian carried out a large buckskin bag filled with serpents, a priest in full dance regalia emerged from a hole in the roof of the Antelope kiva, followed by nine others. They marched to the center of the plaza and stamped on a board to tell the gods of the underworld that the Hopis were about to dance. The long hair of the Antelopes was adorned with eagle feathers, their chins black, white stripes across the mouth from ear to ear. Each arm white to the elbows, each leg white to the knees. Down their chests and backs and along their upper arms from the shoulders down were white zigzags of lightning. They wore necklaces of turquoise, shell, and silver beads, white kilts embroidered with black, a waist sash embroidered in black, red, and green. On each right knee, a tortoise shell, on which was fastened a few sheep and goat hoofs, which made a dull clanking. From their waists hung fox and coyote tails. They shook rattles filled with pebbles and sang. The chief was an albino. "The iris of his eyes were pink, and his hair was the color of new rope."

The Snake dancers moved in columns of three—a carrier, a hugger, and a gatherer. The carrier held a snake in his mouth, his teeth softened with clay to protect the creature. As the carrier danced around the circle, the hugger followed behind with a snake whip ready to guard the dancer's face. After it had been carried around the circle four times, the snake was released and the gatherer swooped down to recapture it. They all danced to the tune of the Antelopes' chanting and rattles and the buzzing of the angry rattlesnakes. After the carrier finished dancing with one snake, he

went back for another. At the end of the dance the chief stepped
to the middle of the plaza, the gatherers circled him with sacred
cornmeal and drew on the ground six radiating lines—to the north,
the west, the south, the east, up to the sun, and down to the underworld. The gatherers threw the snakes in a pile in the circle and
said a short prayer; then the Snake dancers leapt forward, plung-
ing their hands into the squirming mass, each trying to get as many
snakes as possible, some grabbing eight or ten at one time. The
dancers then raced down the mesa trail, carrying the messengers
into the desert and releasing them to carry prayers for rain to the
underworld.

The origin of the snake dance may be linked to the same prolonged drought that depopulated Chaco Canyon and other
Anasazi communities in the 1200s. The version of the story that
Earle Forrest heard from the Hopi went something like this: Tiyo,
the Snake Boy, had been curious where the great river that passed
through their lands went. He built a boat and set off to explore.
The river tumbled him far away to the sea, where he was swept
onto an unknown island. The waters were so swift that he could
not return. While he sat on the shore debating his fate, Spider
Woman came. She fed and comforted him, then crawled behind his
ear to guide him back through the underworld, which was populated with many dangers—bear, panther, wildcat, wolf, and
finally, a big rattlesnake. Each barred the Snake Boy's progress.
But Spider Woman gave him medicine to charm them, until at last
he arrived at the land of the Snake people, who invited him to enter
their kiva and have a smoke. There he saw many snake skins hanging on the wall and the people began to put them on like clothes,
turning themselves into rattlesnakes. Tiyo noticed an especially
pretty woman in the kiva, but when he began to flirt with her, she
changed into a rattler and became vicious. Spider Woman again
came to his aid, giving him a charm that he spat at her, making her
docile and easy to catch. She brought him food and Tiyo was
admitted to the clan. While he lived among the Snake people, he
learned the ritual that would bring rain. They gave him charms and

costumes to make the dance sacred. They gave him the Snake Maiden to be his wife.

Together the couple returned to Tiyo's people, where he was welcomed as one returned from the dead. When his wife became pregnant, she gave birth to young rattlesnakes. They too were welcomed into the tribe, as she had been, until they started to bite the Hopi children who tried to play with them. The people were enraged, driving the snakes and their mother from the village. Then a great drought fell on the land, lasting for decades. Corn withered and died, springs dried up. What had been a homeland of beautiful green grass and trees became a desert. Tiyo, considered a very wise man because of his journey into the unknown, told the tribe that the gods of the underworld were angry because the Hopis had driven Snake Maiden and her children away. However, they could appease the gods, he counselled them, with the ritual he had learned down the great river. The snakes were gathered and washed, prayers and songs of repentance were sung. At sunset, they danced, released the snakes, and waited for rain.

1993. SANTA CRUZ, CALIFORNIA.
The amusement park like an oversized multicolored toy—yellow, turquoise, terra-cotta, white—washed up on the beach. Casino on the beach; parading colonnade and arches. Beach houses range from grand Victorian to Spanish colonial to gentrified bungalow, the northern lip of Monterey Bay curving like a satellite dish into the coast. Neighborhoods spilling over with California hyperbole—leaching mats of ice plant, fluffed-up cushions of white and fuchsia daisies, trumpet vine, and roses as tall as porch roofs—the yards almost artificial in their bounty, groomed in the always right weather. Bait-and-tackle shop, sweatshirts and postcards, surfing museum, 1,001 bikinis. The coastal cypresses stretch leeward, conforming to the push of the prevailing Pacific wind. Along the understruts of the wharf, seals have heaved themselves out of the water to sleep—dozens lined up like snug sardines—one crossways

with his head on the back of another. The tide, pulled low—a big dive now down to the water. I wonder how the hulks got up there. Must be at high tide. Then I see one leap up six feet, catch its flippers on the creosoted beam, and haul its sack of blubber up beside the others. Pups play below in the water, nose to tail to nose, circling and whirling like infinity. At the boat rental booth, men work on an outboard, the mechanic demonstrating the throttle mechanism to two city guys wearing life vests. The mechanic chuckles as they ask him again how it works—"Well, you've got to be smarter than the motor."

I've come, for the third time, to see the monarch butterflies that migrate here to overwinter in the coastal eucalyptus groves. I've been reading for years about these little beauties, and the more I learn about their talents, the more beautiful they become. To see them and to contemplate the intelligence dwelling in their flighty bodies is to feel the force of heroic effort in nature—frailty and tenacity as one. Most of the monarchs living west of the Rockies in any given year journey thousands of miles to cluster high in these weeping branches. Their eastern counterparts travel to sanctuary forests in the central mountains of Mexico. This migratory flight is even more heroic when one considers that a monarch lives only for nine months. It makes the flight once in its lifetime, knowing innately how to navigate the distance because of a speck of magnetite in its head, coded genetic information, and a set of compound eyes that are among the most refined mechanisms in nature. A butterfly's eye has six thousand lenses. It looks like the seeded yellow center of a daisy. No one knows, of course, what it can see—whether images appear as a panorama, mosaic, or fragmented composite—or how far it can see, or how clearly. What's known is that it can perceive motion from all sides and a broad range of colors. The great blue morphos that live high in the tropical rain forest will respond to a scrap of blue silk tethered to a pole, a male attacking the fabric as it would a competing male. Butterflies can see light in the ultraviolet range—glittering opalescence—beyond the spectrum visible to us.

Lepidoptera, the second-largest order in the animal world, have been around for fifty million years—much longer than humans have—and the monarchs have been around for much longer than their California hosts, the eucalyptus trees. These shaggy, fragrant giants were imported from Australia as a source of timber (I once heard that they were brought to be harvested for telephone poles) and have since filled in areas that used to be treeless. The monarchs have found the groves hospitable. By accident, the importation of eucalyptus resulted in this sanctuary. It's hard to imagine how much the monarchs must cherish the forest in which they sleep after their migration. To cherish—not an idea or an emotion—a physical intimacy, the fact of being in the one place they belong. It brings to mind a story my father, an inveterate New Englander, used to tell about the cross-country road trip he and my mother made in the late thirties. There were no interstate highways, few other travelers, barely enough gas stations and cafes to keep them and the old blue Plymouth convertible rolling. He remembered best the places that humbled them—the dirt road through Rabbit Ears Pass in the Rockies, the fearful desert expanse that went on day after scorching day. When they finally got home to the damp and leafy Connecticut forest, he fell to his knees and kissed the ground.

"You're not here to see the monarchs are you?" asks the ranger, after I've snaked along the heavily populated coves to the entrance of Natural Bridges State Park. "They're gone. Only fifteen percent of the normal population showed up, and they left by the end of December."

Usually the monarchs stay into February or March. I drive on— no point in looking at the empty trees—and decide to consult the local expert. John Lane's office in the basement of the Santa Cruz Natural History Museum is a kind of bowerbird nest of books, tropical butterflies mounted in exhibit boxes, computer hum and glow, papers and files—the friendly clutter of a well-used working space. We go outside to talk, leaning against a life-size statue of a blue whale. We talk about our childhoods, the many places we've lived, how few of us get to stay in the same place for more than five years, yet how much we need to feel we're in the right place, connected to the land—rooted, as we say in our tree envy. And how we have to relearn the natural world each time we move— how strange the saguaros and paloverde of the desert are to people like me raised under hickories and maples.

He tells me that some fluctuation in the monarch population is normal. But this year's combination of low population and early departure is not understood. He wonders whether low population itself might be the reason for the departure. Maybe they perceived that a critical mass was missing and said, "Hey, let's get out of here." Like many scientists I've met, he seems to have an abiding faith in nature's unexpected periods of profusion and decline—no catastrophist here, but a pragmatic student of the big picture.

"Is it light sensitivity that normally tells them when to leave?" I ask.

"No, because they do so at different times each year. It's some combination, perhaps having to do with an accumulation of light in their bodies, having to do with the weather, the temperature ..."

Nevertheless, threats to the shrinking islands of wildness that harbor the monarchs are significant enough that California will spend millions this year for habitat protection. Part of Lane's job is consulting on proposed developments to determine whether a planned building site is a monarch habitat. Chalk up one for the butterflies whose presence can ban a condo development. He urges me to go to the El Rosario site in Michoacán, Mexico. You have to go by cattle truck, but it's worth it. You swim your way through butterflies. That site too, however, is threatened. Illegal logging has caused the deaths of millions of monarchs—seventy percent of the 1991–92 population. And by 1993, ninety percent of the original fir forest used by the monarchs had vanished. The remaining trees, though protected by a 1986 presidential decree, are being hacked away. Much of the bootleg logging is done by campesino farmers who use the wood for fuel, sell it, or build their homes with it, then grow crops on the cleared land.

Lane recommends for today that I drive down the coast to Point Lobos and walk the cypress grove before heading back north to the city. Fond of Robert Louis Stevenson's dictum "to travel hopefully is a better thing than to arrive," I drive on. Lobos is a gnarly, moss-draped, wind-stripped stand of trees—barely enough green hanging onto the boughs for photosynthesis. While I'm reading the trail guide, a carload pulls up, checks the billboard—"Oh, it's nothing but trees"—and pulls off. I take the loop trail along the cliff, pass a cobble of stones packed into sedimentary deposits (like pebbles mixed with cement) interbedded with solid rock, the shore crumbling into the hammering waves. I pass a grassy meadow, which the trees have encouraged by providing the shade that stunts more demanding vegetation. Trunks and branches listing away from the wind, gray blighted ice plant collapsed into dormancy. Then patches of wild lilac, the petals of its flower cones so small that up close they look like they're comprised of blue dust, but when I look back from a distance the lilac bloom sprawls like localized oil slicks across the hillside.

Each piece of land can tell a story of grief and loss—forests turned to waste and stone, lifeways dried up in spite of sacred ritual, the human heart ruined by war. And yet the land keeps telling another version of the story—that its cycles and processes are the final authority, that our hearts are constructed to love its beauty. Some land seems too beautiful—the images enter directly to the heart like a patch of nitro taped to the chest. Life enhancing, but what a jolt. So much of California has this effect—the liquid rippling of green grass on the coastal hillsides; live oaks whose wood seems to weave through air the way seaweed weaves through water; the cathedral forest of redwoods, where scorch marks stripe the massive trunks and hollow out the cores, yet the igneous convolutions of bark rise up to random spokes, climb away from the dusk that they are creating, taper, and bud in a slow, green reach for light.

 # CLAIMING THE YARD

AUTUMN. TIME TO CUT BACK THE OVERGROWTH AGAIN.
The pyracantha hedge has gone shapeless as uncombed hair. The
paloverde has pressed a limb against the stucco chimney running
up the east wall of my house. And the bougainvillea has sprawled
beyond its capacity to hold its boughs upright. Even the aloes and
agaves have sent satellite growths out from their roots, the outly-
ers offending my idea of symmetry in the semicircular garden by
the front door. The profusion always surprises me, though I have
had three years to get used to desert living. When I'm not cutting
back and pulling up, I'm struggling to keep alive plants that don't
belong here—peppermint, petunias, tomatoes, and marigolds.
Since the temperature in Tucson has been over one hundred degrees for most of the past four months, my attempts at gardening
look pretty crisp these days. I have mastered only clove-scented
basil. "My basil trees," I call them. The cluster of glistening sweetness has thrived for six months in the backyard shade, growing
three feet tall, sporting woody stalks an inch thick and leaves big
as serving spoons. Though it is already October, I don't have the
heart to whack them down to make pesto.

My friends who know my dreamy penchant for oceans and
woods find it strange that I live in the sun-beaten starkland of the
Sonoran Desert. To be honest, so do I. At times I feel green de-
prived, and I would not be surprised to learn that there exists a
psychic malady that can be cured only by the visual ingestion of
green wildness—a syndrome similar to the one that afflicts the

light-deprived residents of the Pacific Northwest. But I love not only nature's beauty; I love also her weirdness and pig-headed persistence against hostile conditions. And the desert is nothing if not weird and pig-headed. Consider the spadefoot toad that uses its namesake appendages to dig a home underground, lies there without breathing for months—even years in severe drought—absorbing oxygen through its skin, then emerges to feed and breed at the first music of raindrops hitting the soil. Consider the range of desert dwellers requiring venom in order to survive—Gila monster, ten species of rattlesnake, coral snake, scorpion, centipede, tarantula, black widow, brown recluse, and the venomous Colorado river toad known to kill the dog that laps it. Consider the placid saguaro, a cool phallic water cask that takes its sweet time growing—fifty years before it bothers making arms. Living here has been humbling, teaching me that I don't know much about nature after all, that I am no master even of the small domain of my yard.

A yard, anywhere, is an expression of one's relationship with nature, a curious border zone between the wild and the domestic in which we invite nature to come close, but not too close. Nature does not belong in the house. We buy chemical products to keep our space clear of fungi, molds, bacilli, mites, and fleas. Plants can come inside, if they are content to live in pots. We seal basement windows and crawl spaces to keep out feral cats. And, when a crusty cockroach or lacy newt crawls out of the drain into our kitchen sink, we are shocked at its lack of respect for the border we've drawn. The shaping and ordering of the yard is a warning to nature: here dwells human will.

In the desert the conscientious homeowner gives up on lawn, replacing it with gravel and a few pleasingly arrayed arid-land shrubs and trees—Sonoran bird of paradise, oleander, prickly pear, Joshua tree, Chilean mesquite. After the January rains, the gravel sprouts with mustard, wild onion grass, tumbleweed, penstemon, and globe mallow. Most of my neighbors use Rapid-Kill or Round-Up to keep the gravel bare, so that it provides a more attractive background for their shrubs. Gallon jugs of the stuff are sold at grocery and drug stores. Or one can use the preemergents, which one neighbor assured me don't kill anything; they just stop the seeds from germinating. For the first two years I resorted to arduous biannual weed pulling. This fall I decided to let the front yard go wild and see what comes up.

I was inspired to do so by my earlier experiment with Arizona lupines. I had been accustomed to lupines from the Northeast. They grow in manic meadows along the coast of Maine and New Brunswick—startling spires of peppery deep blue, fuchsia, white, and pink quilting the roadsides. The deep blues predominate in most years, though once I saw the fuchsias and pinks take over. Lupines in the Northeast are bigger and more sturdy than most wildflowers; in fact, they are a runaway garden variety, or, as the field guide calls them, "escapes." Shortly after moving to Arizona, I made a road trip north from Tucson to Globe. It was April and I had no idea what to expect from spring in the desert. The route made a gradual ascent from creosote bush and saguaro terrain to one of varied grasses. The shoulder lit up with the burgundy tassels of bromegrass, and then deep blue began to line both sides of the road—a linear bouquet that extended for fifty miles. Pulling off to identify the blooms, I was surprised to discover that they were lupines, smaller in stature and in leaf and flower size, their color more subdued, but morphologically identical to the eastern runaways. A few miles farther on, lupines blanketed entire hillsides and arroyos, the ground tinted as if a cloud shedding a blue shadow had drifted over.

The bloom passed nearly as quickly as a cloud. I returned two weeks later to gather seed and the task was a challenge. Not only had the flowers passed, the plants had become entirely desiccated, blown flat and empty by hot, dry winds. I collected what pods I could find and brought them home to scatter in the yard. The following spring my captives bloomed out of the gravel by my mailbox. When that small wild blue meadow flared up and passed into dross, I began to feel at home.

Though my eagerness to control nature in the borderland of my yard is less developed than that of many of my neighbors, this past summer I was forced by termites to enter the chemical marketplace. There is not much wood on the outside of my adobe house, but it sits on wooden beams all too accessible to the ground-dwelling insects. The queen of a termite colony can lay thirty thousand eggs in a day, so once the drills and sawdust trails are found in the cellar, one tends to leap for corrective measures. In the rush of a busy work week there were miscommunications with the pest people. Before I'd had time to fully understand the treatment plan, what biocide they would use, what risks there might be, what options I had, I came home to find a crew of gloved, goggled, and masked workers pumping something called Dragnet into every seam and crevice that might provide access for the bugs. Things went from bad to worse. The workers drilled through a cement slab and burst a water pipe, which soaked the carpet in my bedroom. By the time I had finished arguing with the company's owner about who was responsible for fixing the mess, the rug had begun to stink of fungus and mold. The carpet man came, made a diagnosis from the stench, sprayed on an antifungal. What is it? I asked him. MBI, he said. What's that? I asked. We just call it a microbiological inhibitor, he said. Does anyone sleep in here? I do, I replied. Well, I wouldn't, he warned. He installed a huge fan under the carpet, clipping down the edges so that the surface waved like Jell-O, and the stink wafted throughout the house. We'd better let that dry for a few days, he said, and left me in the chemical haze.

I admit that I'm among the first to claim our species would be better off if we had a closer relationship with nature—one of understanding rather than exploitation. But this domestic debacle got me thinking that there are limits to the claim. We may need to be close to the song of the mockingbird and the Swainson's thrush because their music wakes up a benevolent part of our minds that is usually sleeping. We may need to be close to the sustaining power of the land because it feeds us body and soul; to trees because they manufacture oxygen and teach us by the example of their long and rooted lives to slow down. We may need the lessons in endurance, in the heroic capacity for healing and regeneration that nature provides. But we need also to distance ourselves from nature—from the random forces that would wreck our health and homes; from the microbial upstarts that would colonize our blood; and from certain tendencies of mind, which are only natural, such as the lust for killing.

The geneticists say that evolution favors complex brains such as ours because our intelligence, at least in theory, enables us to change faster than does the slow dance of genetic selection and drift. But we seem to be too slow for our own ambitions in this regard. Take killing. For thousands of years (a blink in evolutionary time) human beings have lived with a collective moral decision that killing others is wrong. We have decided to kill our killing, to quell that aspect of our animality. Yet a resume for our species would have to report that we haven't come close to accomplishing that goal. Indeed it seems that the three things most troubling to us—violence, sex, and death—all speak of our struggle with our animal nature. Our relationship with nature, both inside our bodies and outside in our yards, is as complicated as our intimate tangles with one another. I guess that's why we like to tame nature by thinking of it as something *out there* that we can visit on the weekend to improve our frame of mind.

Time to cut back the overgrowth again, to stake my claim for order and beauty against the chaos of nature's profusion. While I'm out there whacking and hoeing, pulling up and pruning, cutting down one plant so another will thrive, I'll remember how good that work feels. I get a little crazy when my hands are out of dirt for too long, like my house cats, who climb the windows and walls if I don't let them out to do some killing.

FOUR

 # WOLF, EAGLE, BEAR: AN ALASKA NOTEBOOK

I

ON THE DAY I LEAVE FOR ALASKA, THE EARLY FLIGHT TO SITKA routing through Los Angeles and Seattle is canceled—the city of glitz and gangs smoking from riots after the acquittal of the cops who pommeled Rodney King. Everyone but the jury is convinced that whatever conundrum of the law was argued in the case the outcome had nothing to do with justice. Was it fifty-nine blows with a billy club that were inflicted on the man, drunk and reeling on his hands and knees? I've tried to mimic giving that many blows. After the first eight swings, my shoulder fails me and I'm convinced that only the adrenalin kick of rage could make the assault physically possible. A wasted Black man. Four overworked White cops. Now cities coast to coast have blown open with a reciprocal rage—looting and burning, the dispossessed claiming anything they can grab. Others have responded with stunned despair at the message we've sent to people desperate for the free- dom this country offers. Where in the world haven't people seen the video and wondered where there might be a refuge from violence?

"The problem's visibility," the ticket agent tells me, "hundreds of fires and ...," discreetly faking a gun with his thumb and fore- finger, "you know." Delta's already canceled their next flight. But I'm in luck, Alaska is taking off.

I'm headed for a place I can't imagine. Whatever I've known, loved, and feared about wildland will be changed in Alaska. That's

why any of us go there. To be humbled by its inhospitality—
millions of acres of unmarked forest, unnamed mountains and
creeping glaciers, lakes by the millions thrown like mirror shards
across the green, the last great herds of caribou blowing like
downed leaves across the land, the scragland home of grizzlies and
wolves—human habitation a mere afterthought to the expanded
consciousness of terrain. Wildlands in the lower forty-eight usually
border cities, suburbs, malls, mine tailings, and superhighways.
In Alaska they border more wildland, the edge of an unpeopled
vastness.

How easy it is to drift into the pioneer mind, the relief that one
could leave for good the spoiled cities, that one could start from
scratch and survive by animal wits in the wild—stalking the black-
tailed deer, living for weeks on one kill, sleeping under its animal-
warm pelt, gathering greens when the fiddleheads unfurl, waiting
for fruit until the salmonberries freshen, waiting for warmth
until—in a good year—July. Such patience would be truly to know
where one was—to live in a functional communism with the land,
replacing everything one has purchased with a thing one has found,
hunted, grown, or made by hand. But I will visit for one month one
small offshore island among a thousand in the Alexander Archi-
pelago. How will I know the place? The question recurs in my
mind like a shopping list.

I grew up in rural Connecticut in the fifties, a solitary child
whose best friends were a dog named Bear and the woodland surrounding our house. I tend to think that the template for my love
of nature was formed in that place, on land the details of which I
can conjure more intimately than I can the faces of the few other
children living nearby—bowers of waxy leaved mountain laurel,
blossoming with thousands of tiny pink parachutes in June, the
tawny high-crowned hickories, the rusty-needle carpet beneath
white pines, and Roundtop, the bald mountain at the farthest
perimeter of our land from which a climber could pluck out the
scenic highlights of our town—Sunnybrook Ice Cream Bar, the

sugar maples and trout pond at Avon Old Farms, the languid
Connecticut River, the green velvet golf-patch of the country club,
and in the distance Avon Mountain, soft and blue. A worn-out,
timid mountain, lacking the contours, crags, and grandness that
any traveler to the American West would expect of a mountain
range, Avon Mountain nevertheless served the function of drawing
one's eyes into the lofty distance and leading one to imagine what
powers might dwell there. Dimly present in my mind when I would
gaze into that forested ridgeline on the opposite side of our valley
was the story my father had told me about King Philip—the belea-
guered chief of the Wampanoags who had led an alliance of tribes
into the devastating Indian War of 1675–76.

I suspect every southern New England town with a mountain
in sight claims King Philip, swears that he hid in a cave "right
up there!" while the village below burned and the colonists
were slaughtered. It's true that raids against the settlers were
widespread—by one account fifty-two of the ninety White settlements in New England were attacked and twelve were destroyed
in one year alone. The chief's Indian name was Metacom, or
Metacomet, and he became tribal leader when his brother
Wamsutta was killed, probably by the British, in 1662. Metacom
was only twenty-four years old when he became chief, but he kept
peace for over a decade. As the colonists took over more and more
of the tribal people's hunting grounds, hostility and suspicion
grew. Indians became dependent on British goods and were forced
into land sales that increased their dependency. War flared when a
Christian Indian who had been an informer to the English was
murdered, probably at the order of King Philip. Three Wampanoags were tried for the crime and executed. The Indians inflicted
retaliatory raids on the Whites—towns, men, women, and children
were burned. Whites answered with more of the same. Other tribes
were swept into the flames. Metacom for years had worked to
build an Indian alliance, without much luck. Tribal rivalries and
distrust of his youthful leadership had worked against him. When

the violence threatened all tribal territories, Nipmucks and Narra-
gansetts joined Wampanoags in the cause of survival. Though the
Native alliance kept the body count in their favor for some months,
their weapons and food supply were inadequate compared with
those of the British. Several years earlier, in the period of peaceful
suspicions, King Philip had been brought in by the British for questioning. He had been fined and his tribe forced to surrender their
weapons.

The chief's wit and dignity must have rankled the colonial lead-
ers. Metacom apparently changed his name in order to be in the
same class as King Charles of England, to whom the settlers
deferred on legal and diplomatic matters. Once when the governor
of Boston attempted to negotiate with King Philip, an ambassador
asked why the chief waged war. He replied that "the Governor was
but a subject and that he would not Treat except his Brother King
Charles of England were there."

In the final weeks of the Indian War, King Philip found refuge
in a cave, while the colonists hired deserting Indians to fight off
those holding the last ground. When the chief was captured his
body was drawn and quartered, the limbs parceled out to his enemies, his head mounted on a pole. Defeated Indians, including,
some say, Metacom's widow and son, were sent to slave markets
in the West Indies.

The Indian War of 1675 meant the virtual annihilation of native
people in southern New England. It's not surprising that the collective memory of the good Christian colonists bequeathed to
future generations the image not of the noble chief's head barbar-
ically stuck on a pole, but of him hiding in his cave—a corrupt
Nero fiddling while Rome burned. As a child, however, gazing at
the worn blue mountain where he was said to have spent his last
days, I didn't think of him that way. The Indian, long gone from
our neighborhoods, had become an adventure of the psyche. Part
hero and part monster, he dwelled in a level of consciousness incapable of taking sides. I knew too little history to feel ashamed of

my ancestors' brutality, to feel heartsick at the suffering that had taken place in thousands of actual lives. I knew that a worn blue mountain had the power to call me away from all I did not know into its darkness. What I wanted was a simple thing—to hike up there, to find King Philip's cave, and to see Avon Valley as he might have seen it. I never did that. But in my childish way, I think I already knew that no American landscape could be seen as merely beautiful—that no American landscape could be seen without also seeing the history of violence that has shaped it.

Bear was the golden retriever, born at our house, who became my hiking companion on neighboring trails. It surprises me that my two childhood loves were woods and a dog, because early in my childhood dogs in the woods nearly killed me. I remember nothing of the experience, except the facts from a news clipping and a few inconsequential details—the color, gray-blue, of my jacket, the steep incline of the trail, my father's sweating red neck as he carried me to the car, the tarred driveway of the doctor's office that turned us away, ether smell, a cold metal table—not the violence, not the tenderness that must have brought me back. Perhaps my not remembering means I have never come fully back, though my family describes me as having been a joyful, energetic, outgoing child. I trust the body's wisdom in its forgetfulness.

A friend at seventeen was gang-raped, dragged by the hair from a rock concert into the woods. She, too, remembers nothing significant—her hair caked with mud, most of her clothes missing. The next day she got up, did some more coke, and went to work at her waitress job. Ten years later, after she had finished a Ph.D. in folklore, she walked away from a big academic job to return to the landscape she loved in the Pacific Northwest. Her car was broken into as soon as she arrived, triggering a psychic helplessness that rhymed exactly with her forgotten trauma. That night she awoke in a hotel room certain there was a man in the closet. She searched through it—nothing—but was not reassured. By morning, still panicked, nearly immobile, she crawled along the floor to the phone and called a crisis center. She was diagnosed with post–traumatic stress syndrome—the disorder war veterans experience after the physical, emotional, and moral terrors of combat. Having gone through a rehab program, she now takes comfort in helping the next generation of women through her research, teaching, and writing. But still she does not remember what actually happened during her trauma, only the barest factual report— "I was gang-raped at seventeen, dragged by the hair into the woods ..." Friends have recommended hypnosis so that she might remember more. Why? she asks. Think of what you could write! they say. Why?

At age three I was attacked in the woods by two dogs. I wore a hooded snow jacket and leggings. They could get only my face. At the time my father was a local celebrity because of his popular radio programs and his theatrical community spirit. He emceed talent shows, judged beauty pageants, starred in plays, and broadcast live radio from the county fair with his pet cow, Bessie Bossie. He had many fans who lavished favors—from free ski resort tickets to lemon meringue pies—upon his fortunate family. My trauma, of course, had been on the news. He had heard a whimpering sound and, uncertain whether it was laughter or crying, had come to find me in the woods. He kicked and hurled the two dogs down the hillside and carried me—my ripped and bleeding face against his neck—to safety.

When I came home from the hospital, I remember our car stopping at the mailbox, a jumbo rural aluminum one painted flat black. I remember the box spilling open with hundreds of little pastel-colored envelopes all addressed to me. I think at that moment, receiving those gifts—the words of strangers who wished me well, calling me back from the wild terror into human comfort—I became a writer.

I kept the news clipping for many years. To read it made me feel heroic. I had lived through something I might have died from. My mother didn't like me to talk about it. "It's in the past, dear," she would say to comfort me. But it was not comfort I sought. To remember even the newspaper version meant to me that I was awake.

Bear became my protector. A large golden, his chest was a barrel that amplified his muscular bark. He patrolled the woods eagerly, strutting like a stallion when he had completed his rounds. Thunder was the only adversary that got the better of him. When a storm rumbled into the valley, Bear ran raging through the woods, his barks echoing off Roundtop's granite cliff back down to the house. Like any good companion, he was emotionally attuned, knowing how to snuggle up when one was crying or to lie quietly by the bedside when one had the flu. Once he saved three baby rabbits, carrying them one by one in his mouth to our laps on the porch. We were stunned by his gentleness, even though we knew he'd probably killed their mother minutes before. My brother and I raised the babies in an outdoor cage before turning them loose in some dog-free woods across town. Once when Bear was on the hunt, I ran with him for hours, transfixed by his playful brutalizing of a rabbit. He let the victim hop a few feet ahead of him, then danced his snout down close, jabbed and tore, backed off. Even after the rabbit's guts had spilled out, a glistening gray mass of tubes dragging along on the ground, the little one limped on. The dog seemed to love this part of the hunt, prolonging the kill for the pleasure of the chase. I was glad for Bear that he'd kept his hunting spirit wild. That knowledge felt like a forbidden secret he and I shared.

Bear was also good at killing copperheads. A large den of them lived in a stone pile down by the brook. The first years we lived there, my father shot dozens of them, their bodies looped like rope in a bushel basket. I rarely saw a copperhead alive, but I imagined them everywhere—their smell of kerosene and cucumbers, the hourglass pattern of their red-and-brown skin, the diamond-shaped head, jaws wide to hold the venom sacs. My father was a good shot and even the neighbors called on him to dispatch the

vipers. Bear's method was simpler. One pounce—paws pinning the
tail and head—then a lunge midbody, a quick snap of his neck, and
the snake went limp. Sometimes he shook the carcass back and
forth until it ripped apart. Sometimes his paw would miss the head
and he'd get bitten. The worst of Bear's snakebites occurred one
time when he lunged exactly at the moment the snake rose up to
strike. He took the bite deep in the throat. Though he had lived
through venomous bites before—a success story for the local vet—
this bite was more serious. A baseball-sized abscess formed under
his chin and by nightfall he labored into near coma. The vet came
to the house, lanced the abscess, administered antivenin—all of us
down on our knees talking with that beautiful friend with whom
we couldn't bear to part. "Try to keep him awake," the vet said,
"stay up with him all night." In shifts, we held his head in our laps,
talked to him, stroked his ears, wept and promised he'd be all right.
By morning he was on his feet and ready to patrol the woods. We
hoped the trauma would make him afraid of snakes, but he kept
hunting them. I don't remember him ever taking another bite.
Perhaps his technique became more refined.

As much as I loved those woods, I never walked there unafraid,
without an animal alertness and respect for the territorial bound-
aries that intersected with my own.

The strangest intersection occurred on an overcast autumn afternoon when only my mother and I were at home. Our house was
built into a hillside such that the living room was on the second
floor if one looked out the west windows, but on the first floor if
one looked out to the east. That westward viewpoint was like the
front row of a balcony. The woods below, curving and sloping to
form a deep basin, became a stage on which nature's stories were
played. My mother and I made an annual fall ritual of gathering
mosses, ground pine, partridgeberries, and British soldiers from
those woods. We spread the living room floor with newspapers,
and on our hands and knees built terrariums from this bounty—

microforests sealed into brandy snifters where it would rain and they would grow all winter.

That day we looked out the window to see a timber wolf sitting on the sloping lawn where our trail descended from the woods. Scruffy, peaceful, observant, she turned her gaze slowly to take in the gardens, the woodpile, jalopy and bikes, the lean-to woodshed, the white clapboard house—the complex scent of human lives. How we kept the dog quiet, I don't know. We knew that wolves did not live in Connecticut. Yet here was a wolf sitting in our yard—a fact that no one's doubting would take away from us. When my father came home from work, he didn't believe us. It must have been a German shepherd or a husky. And it is true that the animal's body bore some resemblance to such pets. But that creature's wary calmness was a thing cultivated in the wild. She had come down from Roundtop, from woods to the west and the north—the patchy wilderness that snaked between houses, suburbs, turnpikes, and cities, obliquely connecting our woods with the Catskills, the Berkshires, the Adirondacks, and the great woods of the Canadian north. Winds blew down from there in winter— once bringing snow so deep we shoveled a tunnel, not a path, leading from our front door. The she-wolf sat for a long time, if the time an experience takes can be measured by its impact. Time, always running too fast or too slow, mercifully left us—until the wolf stood up, turned around, and walked silently back into the mystery of those woods.

II

IT IS A RAINY AFTERNOON IN SITKA. THE SKY IS BLUSTERY GRAY. Cold rain. It's May and the days are seventeen blurred hours long. Splatters of granular snow mixed with rain smear against the window, distorting the seaside panorama into little strips of bar code. Forty-seven degrees. I suspect the snow has blown down from the rocky peaks rising abruptly across the road, where this morning the old-growth spruces were sugared with white. The northern rain forest, which typically gets a hundred inches of rain in a year, is so wet that moss grows on sheet metal roofs. Sitkans don't stop for the rain. Little League season opened on a sodden Saturday. And there was a kid's fishing derby on Swan Lake last week, the parents out there drenched, setting a good example. To wait for a clear day here is like waiting for snow in the Sonoran Desert. Last summer, I am told, there was not a single blue sky. Residents of this soaked island learn to be as fluid as the ghostly finger-long slugs that brighten the near-black forest floor.

From my window I watch a bald eagle standing at the water's edge. It seems to be daydreaming into the switchbacks of a tidal stream that etches the mud flats and runs into the bay. Another eagle crosses the first one's airspace, gliding along the shoreline then arcing out over deep water and circling back. This time its flight pattern comes so low that I hear the wind vibrate through its extended primary feathers. A third eagle—not bald at all, the white headdress wet and scruffy—perches on top of the fat spruce on the bank, wings stretched out like a standing cormorant. To dry? Ballast against the gusty wind? For the pleasure of feeling its wings vibrate against the wind without the effort of flying? When the other two fly by (its mate, perhaps, and the speckle-headed off-spring) the treed bird speaks to them, a series of five short trills followed by a longer call, higher pitched than raven or crow. On my list of anticipated wildlife sightings, I hadn't counted on bald eagles at my doorstep.

Why does watching wildlife give us pleasure? More than pleasure, why does it ring the spirit? In the Indian way, an encounter with a wild animal makes a place sacred. I use the word *sacred* timidly, lacking a personal practice of relationship with the divine. I am not a person of faith, rather I am a person of the desire for faith. Yet there are experiences that open a reverent dimension of being. Mircea Eliade says that "the cosmos is so constructed that a religious sense of divine transcendence is aroused by the very existence of the sky." Place a soaring bald eagle in that sky, and only the hardest head could refuse to answer with its own soaring.

Sitka—a town of eighty-four hundred residents, fueled by logging, fishing, and tourism—is the only major settlement in southeast Alaska fronting the Pacific Ocean. It is the only major town on Baranof Island, which is otherwise composed of three thousand square miles of muskeg, old-growth hemlock and spruce forest, ragged tiers of snow-capped crags, perpetual ice fields, and water that leaks omnisciently down from the heights in the form of rivers, streams, falls, trickles, runnels, and drops. The sea interlaces with the land in bays, channels, fjords, coves, inlets, and marshes. In short, water is the language of this country, and the land speaks intimately with the sea.

On this rainy afternoon two immense barges full of pulp, pulled in tandem by a tug, are droning out of Sitka Channel on their way to Japan to become (through an unimaginable alchemy) rayon and cellophane. MAKE JOBS—NOT MORE WILDERNESS reads the bumpersticker on a logging truck, which sums up the local economy. The Alaska Pulp Corporation, operating a mill at Silver Bay, is Sitka's largest employer. Nestled between steep, gorgeous green mountainsides lies the conglomeration of post-apocalyptic buildings, vast vats of scum, stacks puffing out stench, and cargo berths where the economic intercourse goes on night and day. Clear-cuts do not yet appall here as they do when seen by the traveler passing over the shaved body of Oregon, where great wildlands have been reduced to a punk cut. There is still plenty of forest to waste in southeast Alaska, and families, the thinking goes, will need to waste it to thrive. The barges move slowly out of the embrace of the harbor, past the bell buoy, heading north through the last serpentine stretches of the Inside Passage between here and Anchorage.

I have been making a daily walk to town, suiting up from head to ankle in PVC storm-wear. Along the mile of sidewalk between my lodging and the village center lie run-down houses and tidy ones, the hardware store, a McDonald's, the liquor store, the high school with its community swimming pool, the supermarket, and lily-infested Swan Lake. In any town, a kind of intertidal zone exists between what's built up and what's wild, between the domestic and the feral—the scruffy edge of roads and walkways, the parks and back lots, gutters and ditches—where native plants, insects, rodents, birds, and lost pets thrive. Such zones often serve as prologue to what one may find in the local forest and they demonstrate the entrepreneurial prowess with which wild things adapt to changes in the land.

Here the tree trunks, leaves, and mulchy ground are all darkened, intensified by wetness. Yellow wild violets and skunk cabbage flowers blare against the rich black soil. The tissue-paper delicacy of new leaves shines with moisture as if the surfaces have been oiled. Tall salmonberry canes spread a profuse tangle of leaves and muted fuchsia blossoms, which lean out over the sidewalk reaching for open space and light. A rufous hummingbird—cinnamon pelt with a fluorescent pink bib—cozies into one of the blooms and flips its tongue down into the well of nectar. These little packages of hyperbole begin arriving in southeast Alaska from their winter home in Mexico by mid-April. I can't imagine having the strength or the patience to walk from Mexico to Alaska. Yet this creature, which has a metabolic rate so intense it must feed continuously all day and drop into a state of suspended animation to survive the cool night, makes the flight with assistance from nothing other than its minuscule neural network, genetic code, and whatever feeding opportunities occur along the way. The entire journey depends upon coevolved systems—that nectar-producing flowers will be ripening at nearly constant intervals along the flight path.

Perhaps the pleasure I take in looking at the serrated leaves of salmonberry, the muscular packages of skunk cabbage—each morphologically distinct and precise—is a coevolved system of my species with others. Perhaps the perception of beauty and variety in nature is a survival-enhancing capacity, the love of place a trait that strengthens the possibility of survival for my genetic successors. It would seem to be in the interest of any species to know and love its territory—the source of its sustenance. *Biophilia* is the term E. O. Wilson uses to describe this "urge to affiliate with other species." Evolution, as I understand it, is a beautifully complex orchestration of accidents—the mind a design of natural selection. The act of loving is one of the planet's legacies to me, and my articulation of that love, one of my legacies to the planet.

Of course, some hummingbirds do not find nectar-bearing flowers when they need them, some insects drown trapped in the wells of deep blooms. Some human beings, like locusts, decimate the fields that feed them. Violence, both accidental and intentional, is everywhere in nature. As is indifference. Yet living things coevolve with places. Koalas live in Australia, Gila monsters in Arizona, maple trees in New England, and boojums in Baja. Even creatures that migrate, such as the rufous hummingbird, do so with an intricately choreographed relationship to place, relying on successive seasons of bloom as they head north. The human species appears to be coevolving with the entire planet. We can live anywhere, adapting (often pillaging) the environment to meet our needs. Yet we still long for particular places. Our longing is promiscuous—a vestigial instinct—so that documenting our relationship with as many locales as possible gives us a surprising amount of pleasure. When the cruise ships drop anchor in Sitka Channel, swarms of tourists off-load, each one hastening to fix with a snapshot, a videotape, or a postcard some proof of presence in the new place.

The strangest plant growing in the waysides here is devil's club. This week I've watched its elephantine leaves thunder forth from the tops of overwintering stems that snake out of the moist soil beneath Sitka spruce and yellow cedar. The woody gray canes reach up to seven feet tall, some climbing straight up, some drooping in heavy arcs, some weaving horizontally. They bear a fuzz of brittle spines. The devil's club looks like a parody of a plant, something cooked up by Dr. Seuss, as silly as it is beautiful. When a leaf emerges, at first it looks like a crumpled sheet of paper. Then it unfolds, forming several pointed lobes, toothed along the edges, bigger than a dinner plate. The leaves spread out horizontally, none overlapping significantly with another, each greedy for what little sunlight will drift down through the needled forest above. The leaves teeter on narrow stalks, the proportions unlikely yet graceful.

Today, just when I've gotten used to celebrating the rain, the sky blooms with oases of pale blue, the mat of clouds separating into billows, and the gleam of sun hitting the water. And mountains suddenly materialize everywhere. Not a single mountain, nor a single ridgeline of mountains, but a rumpled backdrop of cliffs, snowfields, jagged peaks, and crenulated rock, extending far and wide behind the little cluster of habitations. Across the channel on Kruzof Island, Mount Edgecumbe glitters in sunlight, its rivelled volcanic cone and two-humped sidekick hill visible for the first time during my visit here. I am no Thor or Odin like the men who write the nature books I love. They would strike out for those wild heights and the more dangerous their journey, the greater the wonders of nature they would bring back. Danger has no romance for me. I lack the courage to climb Kilimanjaro, cross the polar ice cap in a dog sled, or even to raft down the Colorado. I will never get intimate with those heights or that wildness. Nevertheless, the image of these sky-writing mountains has entered my imagination and I will take them with me when I leave.

The wildest thing I've found in the town—the thing grown most uniquely and expressively from just this place—is a ragged little plank-and-plywood house on an obscure sidestreet overlooking the fishermen's marina. The facade of this weathered, shabby home is covered with painted and carved images—totemic beings with inlaid abalone eyes, the bodies colored black and red and turquoise. Eagle and Raven, representing the two major clans of the Tlingit people, are depicted from a variety of viewpoints. Under the plastic-covered upper-story window, Eagle and Raven perch beak to beak on a curving branch that joins at their feet and becomes a masklike human face. When I asked a Tlingit shopkeeper about the significance of the two birds, he explained that according to traditional ways a member of the Eagle or Raven clan must marry someone of the opposite clan. Children take on the clan of their mother. He went on to explain that there are two Ravens—one a clan and the other a powerful mythic figure, giver and taker of life, trickster, messenger, clown. Tlingit people of either clan see themselves as Children of the Raven. According to the more northern Koyukon people, Richard Nelson has written, Raven is "good and evil, sage and fool, benefactor and thief—the embodiment of human paradox." Eagle, on the other hand, is always simply Eagle, and while he may be associated with qualities of vision and wisdom, he rarely becomes a character in legend.

Also depicted on the totem house are owls, a barking wolf, open-winged doves at each eave—all constructed of the form-line blocks of color characteristic of Northwest Coast tribal art—and one finely carved, unpainted face ringed with abalone inlays. Under the lean-to shed attached to the house lies a rubble of tools, rusty bikes, old wires and cans. From the rafters hang a dead ruffed grouse and several lush, brown mink pelts.

This workaday expression of traditional art and subsistence living is a relief to see in a community where everyone seems to have come from somewhere else, bearing their complex needs and desires—Russian fur traders, U.S. gold-rushers, oil-boomers, back-to-the-landers, and lately the cappuccino and polar-fleece chic spilling north from Oregon and California. Sitka offers two impressive collections of Native arts—the national historic park with its compelling display of giant totem poles set along a forest trail and the Sheldon Jackson Museum showing Eskimo, Aleut, Athabaskan, and Northwest Coast tribal arts. Yet the ramshackle totem house conveys a sense of the ongoing ritual importance of art in daily life, while the story-poles, masks, skin jackets, gut bags,

and button blankets in the collections—beautiful as they may be—
have become artifacts, dead to their sacred or mythic meanings.

These collections do, however, serve as vessels for history.
Sheldon Jackson founded the Presbyterian Mission in Sitka in
1878. His interest in collecting historic and cultural artifacts from
Native people led him to travel extensively along the Alaskan
coast. He brought back braining stones and seal calls (sticks with
seal claws attached to imitate the scratching sound of a flipper on
ice); ceremonial capes and blankets; tiny baskets made of fish skin;
shirts made of mesentery, stitched with sinew threads; wood,
feather, bone, quill, and rawhide masks. On every item the words
PRESENTED BY SHELDON JACKSON are carved and inked in black—
here on a pipe stem, here written across the breast of a translucent
ceremonial skin suit, here on the back side (mercifully) of a
wooden caribou mask. I imagine Jackson camped out in the bush,
a horde of Native arts walled up between him and the cold. In the
small glow of his candle he bends reverently over the wooden mask
of a human face—a carved wreath of leaping salmon encircling the
features. His missionary work has begun. He cuts the delicate
script of his name again and again late into the arctic night. He
loves each mask, its beauty and workmanship, its once ritual
power. He loves trying to imagine what each object once meant—
and with his inscription he ensures, in the name of his god, that it
will mean that no longer.

I think of this desecration whenever I begin to feel inadequate
about my intimacy with nature, whenever I feel that I haven't gone
far enough into it (read, "away from people"), whenever I feel that
I lack the courage to encounter nature-in-the-rough, or that my
interests have been merely womanly and therefore more connected
with the domestic than with the wild. Why add to the sadness that
comes in the wake of heroic tasks, the global elegy that the last
mountain has been conquered, the last lost tribe discovered, the
last great forest turned into rayon socks? I want to become intimate with nature by gazing out my window, taking a daily walk,

studying dandelions and horsetail, watching the bristle-faced otter swimming on its back or the manic western sandpipers drilling for sand fleas, and by attending to the roadside eagle's various calls.

This cavalcade of daily visitations connects me to the place I'm in, each perception a fiber weaving a common fabric of divergent lives. Yet it gives a false sense of intimacy, a coziness of scale that denies the vastness and remoteness of Alaska. One fifth the geographic size of the remainder of the United States, the population of the Last Frontier is less than that of the city of Tucson, less than one person per square mile. Even Alaska's cities are remote and isolated, many connected by jet service, but not by roads. It's easy to forget where I am and think of Sitka as a small island—the town is a seven-mile clump of habitation on three thousand wild square miles of Baranof Island. And this is the diminutive part of the state—a scattering of islands nestled against the Canadian coast. Northwest of here, rugged land extends unbroken by roads for thousands of miles.

The state has suffered its share of explore-and-exploit frontiersmen. Contention over the northern oil fields and the southeast ancient forest is no less dire here than similar conflicts elsewhere on the shrinking planet. Perhaps it is more dire, since the Alaskan economy is defined by limited options, high prices, the demands of a severe climate, and the ideal of individual freedom for which settlers still move to Alaska. The desire to escape urban ruin and the complexities of the collective find their form in the bush, where a family might live fifty or a hundred miles from any neighbor. I watched a TV show about a Minnesota man who ran to the far north after high school, lived the harsh freedom of which he had dreamed, marrying an Eskimo woman who taught him the necessary skills for living off the land. They had what comforts they needed—a handbuilt rough-cut house and an old wringer washer in the yard, which they ran with a gas-powered generator the size of a chainsaw. Their dream was to have a piano and they planned to drag one upstream by canoe to their homestead. Whether out picking berries in the summer or setting deer meat to store in a cache, they each wore a revolver strapped to the waist for bear protection. They longed for the bush plane that would deliver mail once a month, for the radio's precious gossip of other bush families—*The McLains are back from a month in Anchorage and they send their love to ... Sabra T. reports that her traps are set and she's begun running the hundred-mile loop in her dogsled ... News for Jimmy Skultka, your tar paper and nails will arrive on ...* A teacher came on the mail plane every several months, weather permitting, to bring a learning kit for the parents to use in educating their children at home. The toughest hardship for them was not the struggle for food and warmth, but their isolation—their hunger for connection with others.

I read this need as good news. That old frontier ideal of escape and heroic individualism seems, at best, anachronistic on an overcrowded planet—at worst, our species' fatal moral flaw. Walter Brueggemann writes that "*place* is space with historical meanings" and that while "pursuit of space [as the arena for freedom] may be a flight from history, a yearning for place is a decision to enter history ... to be in a place somewhere and answer for it and to it." To see Alaska as a *place* is to see the eagle, grizzly, humpback, caribou, glacier, forest, tundra *and* to read the news that the suicide rate among Native (Koyukon, Athabaskan, Tlingit, etc.) men in their twenties is ten times the national average. Such is the hopelessness that successive rushes of frontier freedom have spilled upon this land.

Satin tonight, the water, where hours earlier an otter scurried out to feed at low tide. A hazy moon hangs above the channel, shedding timid light in the halftone northern spring sky. I cannot get out of my head the spectacle of twenty bald eagles that earlier had stood like sentries along the gravel shore, not bothered by the traffic of island people whirring by on their way to and from work. What brought them to converge in this place? They were not feeding, or claiming territory from another species. A few idly plucked at weeds washing up on shore. They appeared purposeful, attentive, patient—as if this place were the only one in which they wanted to be. Earlier, out on the tidal flats, one eagle had struggled and squawked for hours, its talons stuck in the meat of a large salmon. It must have shaken or eaten its way free, for the commotion finally ceased. The mass of eagles arrived soon afterward, leading me to think they'd been attracted by their compatriot's ordeal. Other animals behave that way. One theory, for example, about the mass strandings of pilot whales on Cape Cod is that if one whale becomes deranged and beaches itself, dozens will follow, dumping themselves on shore in solidarity. Was this the case with the eagles—the call of the distressed one, a beacon to others of its species? The place made sacred to them by the suddenly apparent riskiness of life?

III

A BEAUTIFUL SPRING DAY, WARM AND PARTLY SUNNY. AT SIXTY-five degrees Sitkans break out their tank tops and shorts. After a week of this atypical weather, everyone in town is high on the freedom of the outdoors. Joanne, Carolyn, and I decide on a hike up the Indian River Trail. We meet at the bookstore and, while we browse and chat with the owner, overhear the announcement on the radio that a brown bear has been sighted near the trailhead just where we had planned all week to hike. Two visitors and one local—a sizing-up. We defer to Carolyn, the local, who makes no bones about it—she's not comfortable knowing there's a bear in the area. What if we didn't know? If we hadn't come into the store and heard the broadcast? But we did and we have. And it is May—the month when the bears wake from hibernation. The thought of crossing paths with a thousand-pound grizzly who hasn't eaten or taken a shit for six months, and may have hungry cubs bothering at her side, is enough to convince me that we should change our plans. But I'm reticent to say so, not wanting to appear lacking in courage. Wildlife researchers estimate that there are 150,000 brown, black, and polar bears in Alaska. That makes the distribution a little more than one bear for every three human inhabitants. Here in the southeast as many as 8,000 brown (or grizzly) bears populate the islands strewn between Ketchikan and Yakutat, in some areas living as densely as one bear per square mile. They thrive in the region, fattening on spawning salmon in the fall and finding the winters so moderate that some years they don't bother to hibernate at all. Knowing that the browns live here brings out an alertness and caution in some people, an aroused state of curiosity in others, and a challenge to the predatory instinct in yet others. No one can ignore the bear. One either hungers to encounter one or not to. And when I ask, "Should I be worried about the bears?" everyone has a bear story to tell.

The man who runs the sporting goods store tells me I'd be lucky ever to see a brown bear. He assures me I'm more likely to be killed by a mosquito or by tripping on a root than to be harmed by a bear. His wife tells me that she fears them—that a friend of theirs lost some leg muscle to a bear. "Of course," she qualifies the danger, "the man had been hunting and he had half a deer slung over his back." The woodsmen tell me that a brown bear will never attack unprovoked. But what is one to think about the respect for life of a species that, the biologists claim, will routinely hunt down and kill its own cubs? Someone else tells of the man hunting alone at the southern end of Baranof Island—"All the search party found were his boots ... and his feet were still in them." "Hang bells on your pack," says one eavesdropper. "Don't carry food," says another. "Don't go in the woods when you're menstruating," the women say. The men tend to laugh when they tell bear stories, the women to look earnest. Others take the bear's side—telling with contempt of rich hunters from the lower forty-eight who charter a private plane and backcountry guide, down a brown bear and take only the claws as evidence of the kill. All bear partisans prefer the seriousness and respect with which Native people traditionally end an animal's life—eating the meat and the brain, making rope of the gut, a shirt of the mesenteries, a blanket of the hide, a necklace of the teeth and the claws.

We decide to drive by the house of a friend who is both hunter and naturalist, one who has spent more time in the wildlands than in town, and whose judgment we trust. He is sober about the danger of bears and provides us with an aerosol can of capsicum—the chemical that makes chili peppers hot and that has been marketed recently as a bear deterrent. It works only if sprayed from a distance of ten feet or less. In some cases, it merely serves to enrage an already testy animal. And he tells us his scariest bear story. While deer hunting in a remote forest of a remote island, he noticed fresh bear tracks underfoot. He quieted his dog, readied his gun, and walked on, deciding to follow the track. When he found himself circling back on his own tracks, he realized that the bear was stalking him. He stood still. There was quiet. Then his dog let loose the yelps only a bear could arouse; the bordering woods erupted with rampage, an ungodly roar ripping the air as the animal tore through the scrub. In a rage of ferocious proportion, the bear stormed back and forth at the edge of the muskeg. The hunter, locked in place, knew that even his rifle would be worthless if the bear decided to charge. But strangely it did not. It drew the territorial line with its anger, then pounded off into deep woods.

After this tale, the aerosol can strapped to Carolyn's knapsack provides me with little reassurance. Having known the terror of tooth and claw, I'm not titillated by the threat of enduring such an experience again—or a worse one. It's all well and good for Robinson Jeffers to rhapsodize about being eaten by a red-tailed hawk—"what an enskyment; what a life after death." I'll admit there is romance to the notion of my genetic material living in the ecosystem more freely and wildly than I, as a human being, would dare to do. But I prefer sticking around with my domestic companions to experiencing the enwildment of being eaten by a bear. My bear story, I begin to realize, soon will intersect with everyone else's like ripples on a pond.

"The Koyukon people," Richard Nelson writes in *Make Prayers to the Raven*, "have great respect for the unpredictability, aggressiveness, tenacity and physical power of brown bears. Unnecessary encounters are strictly avoided, and any approach to them is made with utmost caution, very different from the confidence hunters show in pursuing the milder, more predictable black bear. When a man comes across brown bear tracks on the fall snow, he is likely to leave the area immediately. People emphasize that this is a very difficult animal to kill, that a man alone could shoot it many times and still be attacked."

Special prohibitions govern the Koyukon woman's relationship to the brown bear. She must not eat the animal's meat and she must take care never to breathe the steam from the cooking bear meat. Violating the taboo would make a woman mean, insane, or ill, so great are the spiritual powers of the animal. She could not hunt them, should look away if one came into her sight, and she should not speak the animal's name.

We decide to steer clear of the bear sighting and take the shorter hike to Beaver Lake. We drive out past the pulp mill to a scrappy backwoods parking lot. The trail starts out as a steep course of switchbacks, reinforced on the most severe inclines with rough-cut timber stairs. Huge cedars, the tallest I have ever seen, and hemlocks climb the mountainsides below and above us. Beyond— steeper faces of sheer mountain, fractured peaks, silver blades of snowmelt slicing down through rock, snowpack blotching the high rocky crests. Topping the ridge, the trail levels off into muskeg and our breathing begins to relax.

A narrow boardwalk leads out from under the dank cedars across a grassy meadow. A scattering of blossoms brightens the field—clusters of yellow skunk cabbage, white bunchberries, and a single fuchsia orchid no bigger than a deerfly (a Jeffrey shooting star?). In the mud patches along the trailside appear clean tracks of the day's prior traffic—pointed deer hooves, waffled hiking boots, and dog paws. The farther into the woods we hike, the quieter we get. Quiet draws the forest closer, as if by stilling the mind's busy language center some vestigial territorial sense comes back to us. Why should I feel such pleasure to be in the wilds? Some inarticulate kind of memory calls me—not a personal memory, but something deeper—perhaps a species memory, a cellular sense of human origin. Emerson said it: "The mind loves its old home."

About a half mile out on the muskeg, we start single file into another shadowed cedar grove, the heady scent inviting. Suddenly, *bear* enters my mind—a ripping and real presence that sees me as either danger or food. The others move on ahead. I stop and stare at the dark wet mud to the left of the boardwalk. The boggy ground is a perfect medium for making an accurate textbook animal track—except this print is three-dimensional. The massive pressure of the animal's weight makes a bowl of the pad. Five oval toe marks press above it into the mud, above the toes five deeply gouged claw scars line up in a row. Brown bear. Black bear track would show claw marks closer to the toes and spread in an arc. The track is fresh. Water has not seeped into the print nor have the edges softened. The bear has left at the sound or the scent of our approach.

Never have I wished more to be without fear, to be the old Tlingit woman I read about who flipped the bears off with a switch of alder. Clearly the bear's track was headed away from us. But I couldn't stop thinking that fear might not be the bear's only response to our presence. What if her cubs gamboled obliviously into our midst? What if, in her winter-long hunger, one of us three women looked like the most delicious thing, and the slowest on our feet, for miles?

Among my tribe—the children of science—fear is a thing to resist and control. As far back into our tradition as I've looked, from the Book of Proverbs to Montaigne to Thoreau, I've found an echo of Franklin Roosevelt's well-heeled one-liner—"The only thing we have to fear is fear itself." As if all human fear were an emotional error, rather than a survival-enhancing product of evolution. Women in our culture understand and respond to fear differently than men do. For one thing, we face it more often, since we inherit a historical legacy of men's social and physical power over us. Fear is our radar. Walking alone down a city street at night or answering our own door to greet a stranger, we make a quick assessment and chart the appropriate course. It is not a question of overcoming fear so much as attuning the instrument of perception so that we can detect a real danger in time to avoid it. Street-smart fear is a woman's friend and companion.

A woman carries that emotional resonance with her when she goes to the woods. A man, we are taught to believe, goes to the woods to test his courage—scaling the heights, running the rapids, hooking and shooting the prey, downing or at least facing down the brown bear. A woman goes to the forest not to face her fear, but to escape it. She picks berries, mushrooms, mosses, and vines. If she imagines building a cabin there, she pictures its garden, its window boxes, and its raggedly domestic yard—not the moose rack mounted over the front door, not the revolver she will carry when berrying in bear country. But no matter how sweet and pastoral her longing for the wild, once there, she finds her old companion fear has come along. One woman tunes her radar to the psychopathic mountain man, another to the rampaging bear.

"Hey, you guys," I whisper ahead to the others. "Look at this." We all lean over the bear's imprint, quietly taking in the detail and remapping our sense of the territory.

On our way back down the trail, I take the lead, embarrassed by my eagerness to depart—but not so embarrassed as to change my mind. I wonder whether the others would have gone on if my concern had not been so apparent. Neither Carolyn nor Joanne had tried to cajole me onward, and I feel grateful that there is room in our friendship for an honest fear. We brush past the overarching devil's club, the alders fully fledged with new leaves, the salmonberry canes dropping their pink flowers to form green nuggets of proto-fruit.

I've read that early humans shared caves with hibernating bears and stacked cave-bear skulls in high-mountain sanctuaries. But since then the relationship between *ursus arctos* and *homo sapiens* has taken a dive. Our interactions now seem limited to two— avoidance or slaughter. Friendships that cross the borders between species are not impossible. The covenant between people and dogs is so strong, archaic, and cellular (lodged in our respective chromosomal codes) that it can transcend, as in my own case, traumatic experience that suggests canines are not to be trusted. Far more children die or are maimed each year by dog bites than from bear attack. Yet the attraction between human and canine species remains. So important was the dog to the ancient Egyptians that Anubis—the god of death, master of mummification, companion to the soul in death—was portrayed with the head of a jackal. The dog appears with Diana or Artemis as companion on the hunt, as mediator between the domestic and the wild, the earthly and the divine.

The friendship between people and dogs continues to be, even in our dense urban constellations, the most affectionate connection between our species and another. What other animal is so welcome in our homes, so responsive a companion, so interested in understanding our language and moods, so capable of bringing out playful, patient, and nurturing qualities in us? Konrad Lorenz speculated about how this friendship developed during the lives of our earliest ancestors. Jackals may have followed in the tracks of hunting parties, scavenging for spoils once the people had eaten their fill and made camp for the night. "The stone-age hunters," writes Lorenz, "must have found it quite agreeable to know that their camp was watched by a broad circle of jackals which, at the approach of a sabre-toothed tiger or a marauding cave-bear, gave tongue to the wildest tones." Perhaps on one restless night, a

Neanderthal, unable to sleep because of his fears, got up and lay a trail of scraps leading toward his camp to draw the jackals near, knowing that if the pack slept soundly, the people could do the same. In the geologically slow motion of evolution (combined with the fast-forward of human will), that action led to poodles, Dobermans, and golden retrievers. It is our heritage to feel safe (already safe in our armed and alarmed urban homes) when we see a resting animal.

These days when we think and talk about our relationships with other animals, we never get much beyond questions of survival and turf. Which creature deserves its livelihood more, the spotted owl or the Oregon logger? It seems a given that we cannot stop the accelerating loss of species and, as those that remain are crowded onto shrinking islands of wildness, our questions become more godlike and less considerate of the godly complexity of nature. Should we shoot the coyote to save the whooping crane, kill the arctic fox to save the Canadian goose? We save the freeze-dried tissue samples of the extinct ones, so far only imagining the biotechnology that might bring them back to life.

RECIPE FOR A DINOSAUR:
A. Find a bead of amber that contains a blood-sucking insect from the age of dinosaurs.
B. Extract genetic material from the blood cells, preserved in the bead, of a bug-bitten dinosaur, and amplify the DNA using the polymerase chain reaction technique.
C. Process and inject into the embryo of an alligator.
D. Wait until it hatches.

—*New York Times,* June 25, 1991

I suppose that to revive the dinosaur would be a kind of friendship with that species. After all the damage people have caused on the planet, any act of kindness will improve the value of our biological stock in the world. But I wonder what kind of planet we might live on now if the human project (not the rhetoric of our project) had been friendship, rather than greed.

We drive to another lake, this one accessible by car over a primitive dirt road. Blue Lake is not as wild a picnic spot as we had hoped for. A man follows us on foot, down the final rutted incline to the water's edge, carrying an outboard motor over his shoulder. Beer and McDonald's trash, five or six fishermen dot the bouldered shore. The water is clear blue-green, fed by waterfalling mountain streams, riled by a stout wind, slapping the rocks, harboring thousands of unseen life forms, too cold to enter, too beautiful not to wish to. We settle for the battered wildness, a little sorry for ourselves, unpack our lunches and eat.

I am glad to have left the high woods to the bear. I imagine the music that such a forest might have sung to me and I am sorry never to have heard it. But it's beautiful to think that a moody creature walks there, one so powerful its presence made us hasten away. I am glad to have left the mark of my scent in her brain, as she has left the mark of her paw in mine. Focusing a zoom lens would not have made me feel closer to her wildness. Whatever constitutes my scent in the mind of a bear is lumbering along the muskeg up by Beaver Lake. She and I exist as interruptions in each other's afternoon, and that is close enough to knowing her for me.

THE NATURE OF POETRY: POETRY IN NATURE

RECENTLY I HAVE BEEN TRYING TO ATTEND TO NATURE in a careful fashion, have tried to strip away my conscious preconceptions and to listen for the most forceful statements nature might make to me. My motive has been to get away from seeing nature as the idealized other, and human beings as the dysfunctionals of the natural world. I have been looking for a more integrated view that admits that chaos and destruction, moral and aesthetic order exist everywhere in nature, that these forces are embedded in us, as we are embedded in the ecosystem. We don't yet know nearly enough about nature—it truly is an inexhaustible mystery. The snares of my attention caught this prey: hanta virus, bald eagle, 111 degrees. Let me elaborate.

At least eighteen people have died during the spring of 1993, many of them young and previously healthy, most of them living on Navajo lands in northern New Mexico and Arizona. An unknown disease, flulike and rapid, has taken them. The public health detectives and the tribal medicine people have puzzled and postulated, working intently to find and allay the cause. Several theories have been floated, but the most likely is that a new strain of hanta virus spread by rodent droppings has evolved in the area. The tribal elders suspected the disease was related to piñon nuts, which have been much more bountiful than usual this year because of a winter of record high rainfall. Since desert rodents thrive on piñons, deer mice and pack rats have been bountiful as well, thereby increasing the possibility of contact with people. Nature, this phenomenon reminds me, is ceaselessly improvising, adopting new forms that incorporate the available material. Nature has no sympathy for individuals, no preference among species. Everything is food for fodder (including young and hearty members of the apparently dominant species) in the great collective appetite of evolution.

Last week I attended a symposium in Alaska at which I was swept into the white water of collective thinking about our relatedness to nature and the precarious waterfall toward which our species intently paddles. Between the heady sessions (how can we get loggers and environmentalists to talk to one another? how can we reimagine our innocence?), I'd walk outside to watch bald eagles cruise the sky, this one calling to its mate, another carrying in its talons a two-foot-long twig to tuck in its nest in the high crown of a Sitka spruce. The paradox was not lost to me that I had flown thousands of miles—paying a huge corporation to consume fossil fuels and dump their rank residue into the atmosphere—so that I could watch eagles and speculate about right relationship with nature. This is how all of our problems look these days— everything is embedded in everything else so that the degree of complication makes us feel hopeless. It's "their" fault, we say—the loggers, the Republicans, the capitalists, the philistines. And yet when we look soberly at our own appetites and habits, each of us is a strand in the tangled web. Our problems are as delicately interwoven as are the relationships between ourselves and the microbes that live in our guts. Nature—the biotic community of earth—in all its beauty, complexity, ugliness, violence, and versatility is connectedness. Connectedness is *our* nature. Yet we never satisfy our hunger for connectedness with one another or with our own fleeting experience. We are nature hungering for itself.

When I returned home to Arizona, the temperature was 106 and everyone reported how it had peaked a few days earlier at 111. My five California sycamores had gone into a leaf drop that looked like fall. Suffering from the heat, the dryness, and an opportunistic infestation of whiteflies, they looked desperate and out of place. I called the tree doctor, who drilled cores into the trunks, sinking implants of insecticide and iron into the wood. Sycamores really are out of place in Tucson. They prefer to grow at higher elevations and nearer to constant water. Here they must endure six months without a drop of rain and with the beating of ferocious sunlight. But given some modest attention, they manage to live and to provide a flickering canopy of leaves over my side yard that would be difficult to part with. By contrast, the paloverde is well adapted to this fierce climate and its survival strategy is a testament to the entrepreneurial nature of nature. Having broad leaves in the desert is not a good idea, because surface area increases the evaporation of precious moisture. The paloverde has solved this problem by developing long needlelike leaves that conserve water. The delicate leaves, however, do not provide enough chlorophyll for efficient photosynthesis, so the tree has developed green bark enabling it to photosynthesize all along its trunk and branches. This seems stunningly intelligent to me and testifies that at least here in the Sonoran Desert the land's desire to produce vegetation is too passionate to be quelled by mere centuries of drought. Nature displays such unlikely persistence in numerous inhospitable habitats.

What does this have to do with poetry? I think it has everything to do with poetry, because art is quite simply another of the products of the natural world, and one of the more honorably humble products of our species. As John Haines writes, "There is nothing in this *mind*, this imagination, this capacity for thought, that does not find its source, its example and inspiration, in the natural world.... [Nature] is, to say it yet another way, the great book we have been reading, and writing, from the beginning." And the three characteristics of nature that my recent observations yielded seem particularly apt to a discussion of poetry. First, poetry is the invention (and reinvention) of form using what materials are available. Forms evolve as our sense of reality changes, capturing a glimmer of the shape of the mental and emotional experience characteristic of a given time in history. As Adrienne Rich writes, "I don't want to know / wreckage, dreck and waste, but these are the materials." Second, poetry is an expression of our hunger for connectedness. We write to cross the borders that separate us from others. And in the solitary process of writing, we feel selflessly connected to an ideal reader, or as Charles Wright said it, to the better part of ourselves. And third, poetry displays an unlikely persistence in a culture that is, at best, indifferent to it. To put it metaphorically, poetry is the stubborn grass that grows between the cracks in the sidewalk.

One of our most dangerous post-Edenic cultural beliefs is that we are separate from nature, exiled from the instinctual paradise of natural order and balance. I don't mean that we are incapable of experiencing the beauty of coastal marsh grass or the grace of a breaching humpback. I mean that immediately after those ecstatic encounters in which we exclaim "Look at that!" to our companions, there is a sigh of dismay or grief. The lives of plants and animals seem blessed by survival instincts, while our lives (examined as a planetary phenomenon) seem to be a disaster. We know our species to be greedy, genocidal, war-mongering, wasteful, and apparently incapable of serving as custodians of the future. We are the ones who have thrown nature out of balance. We need no further evidence that this is the case. And we can no longer run away from our ruin in search of new wilderness—that great American story our ancestors carried with them from Europe. That story is over. We need a new one. Are we smart enough to reimagine ourselves? I don't know. No one knows. This is the essential tension and question of our time.

John Haines also has said that there is no progress in nature or in art. I think that he is right. John Ashbery's "Self-Portrait in a

Convex Mirror" does not supersede the cave paintings at Lascaux. We do not supersede the dinosaurs. Each being, each period of flowering and decay is nature's patient response to the circumstances of the time. When something goes wrong in nature (a volcano or asteroid spewing debris into space and darkening the sun), species die out. We are the first creatures to know that this has happened to other species and may happen to us—*will*, eventually, undoubtedly happen to everything on earth when the sun in its death throes expands to become a white dwarf, drying the oceans and melting mountains into lava. This physical ending to life on earth is the toughest metaphysical challenge, since most of us lack a faith sufficient to protect us even from our individual deaths. We make art and things that proclaim loudly, "I are here! I have substance!" But we lack a story of who we are that would make us feel at home in our skins. Our faith in nature is insufficient. We believe it will be a moral failure if our species goes extinct. But nature will simply be clearing the way for the next invention, opening a new blank notebook—or, more accurately, reworking the notes she has taken thus far. How do we live with the complexity our lives have become?

I think poems and stories can help. From *Aesop's Fables* to *Jurassic Park*, we have looked to nature, and especially to the lives of animals, to teach us about moral order. And if we lack anything, it is a clear sense of moral order. James Merrill speaks of:

> Stories whose glow we see our lives bathed in—
> The mere word 'animal' a skin
> Through which its old sense glimmers, *of the soul.*

So I want to move on to talk about some poems that offer that glimmer and that I believe have something to contribute in terms of reimagining ourselves as not the dysfunctionals of the natural world, but as its custodians. Whatever we believe about nature and ourselves is always a story, a version of the truth as told by a specific narrator. Art should be helpful, useful. It should enhance our ability to commit acts of will when they are required. And reimagining ourselves clearly requires acts of will.

In "Leaves of Grass" Walt Whitman writes:

> I think I could turn and live with animals, they
>   are so placid and self-contained,
> I stand and look at them sometimes an hour at a
>   stretch.
>
> They do not sweat and whine about their
>   condition,
> They do not lie awake in the dark and weep for
>   their sins,
> They do not make me sick discussing their duty
>   to God,
> No one is dissatisfied—not one is demented
>   with the mania of owning things,
> Not one kneels to another, nor to his kind that
>   lived thousands of years ago,
> Not one is respectable or industrious over the
>   whole earth.

This excerpt *celebrates* the split of which I've spoken—that human beings are essentially separate from nature and animal beings. I love the poem for its longing for the innocence of animal life and for its critique of human malcontent and striving. Whitman even ridicules our more noble pipe dreams—to be respectable and industrious—because, I infer, our striving is so ceaseless and judgment laden. The poem seems to say that we are an error in nature—or at least that we lack the equanimity with our own natures that animals embody. The poem idealizes animals for their very lack of moral responsibility.

Rather than separating human from animal beings, hence from nature, Chilean poet and activist Cecilia Vicuña writes an equation in which *poem* equals *animal*. The poem in its entirety reads:

> The poem is the animal
>
> Sinking its mouth
> in the stream

She defines the animal moment specifically and lyrically. It is important to note that it is not the poet sinking her mouth in the stream—but the poem itself that has gained a life of its own, become animated as a creature in the natural world, a product of evolution, and must quench its thirst.

I've separated (how human of me) the remaining poems I want to talk about into three groups. The first are poems of natural observation in which the author pays careful attention to an animal behavior. In this fashion, the work has something in common with the field notebook of a natural scientist—but the poems have an added dimension, moving from observation to suggest parallels to how we live our lives.

Greg Pape's poem "The Jackrabbit's Ears" begins with a fable-like question, similar to Kipling's *Just So Stories*.

> Why do jackrabbits have such big ears?
> I always thought it was because
> they liked to sit in the shade
> of a creosote bush or a juniper
> all day and listen to God
> or whatever devil might be hungry
> and headed their way.
> That's what I do when I sit
> at the desk waiting for the spirit
> to move me, looking for words
> to say whatever it is that needs
> to be said. I envy the jackrabbit
> his patience and his instinct.
> I admire his big ears, ears
> the light passes through, ears
> that radiate the heat of his body
> and cool him without loss

of water, ears he holds erect
at an angle of seventeen degrees
from the north horizon, pointed
precisely at the coolest area of sky,
listening for the exact sound
of the present, and for the life ahead.

Pape's critter lives in a real, geographic terrain where there are creosote and juniper bushes. His observations are precise—right down to the exact angle at which the rabbit's ears incline to pick up a distant sound. But this jackrabbit also lives on a moral ground where God and devils are forces in its life. Pape equates the rabbit's ears and how well evolved they are for their job with the poet's imagination. The poem thereby dignifies the animal and humbles the human. In this leveling assessment, it offers a post-colonial, post-Columbian view of nature.

Rodney Jones, like Whitman, speaks of the characteristic differences between human and animal beings in "Shame the Monsters." Unlike Whitman, who ridicules his own kind and would like to send us back in evolutionary time to some state of pure instinctual bliss, Jones takes on the complexity and vulnerability of our current inner lives and dilemmas.

It is good, after all, to pause and lick one's genitalia
To hunch one's shoulders and gag, regurgitating lunch,
To mark one's curb and grass, to bay when the future
        beckons from the nose,
Not to exhaust so much of the present staring into the flat
        face of a machine
Not to spend so much of the logic and the voice
        articulating a complex whimper of submission,
But to run with a full stomach under the sun, to play in the
        simple water and to wallow oneself dry in the leaves,
To take the teeth in the neck, if it comes to that,
If it comes to little and lean and silent, to take the
        position of the stone, even to hide under the stone,

But not to ride up the spine of the building with the acid
    scalding the gut,
Not to sit at a long table, wondering
How not to howl when the tall one again personifies the
    organization ...

While Jones critiques our technological and organizational ways, he makes at least this reader feel a tenderness toward our human limitations. When he opens the second stanza with the entreaty "Dear Mammals, help me, the argument with flesh is too fierce ...," he seems to say that he loves us all for our animal need for one another. The poem closes with these stunning lines:

Better to take the mud in the hands and holler for no
    reason, to praise the strange
Alchemy of mud and rain: there is sex; there is food.
It is good to say anything in the spirit of hair and breasts
    and warm blood,
And not to deny the private knowledge, not to wonder
    how not to speak of death,
And not to deny the knowledge of death, not to invent the
    silence,
Not to wonder how not to say the words of love.

By opening the poem with the unselfconscious behavior of animals licking their genitalia and ending with the difficulties of human love, Jones frames the evolutionary distance we have come. I'm touched by the ambivalent nature of that last line as it speaks of how different the animals are from us, how much better their lives are in many ways—"It is good ... not to wonder how not to say the words of love." I don't fully understand what he means by that. I make two possible readings—perhaps there are others. It's true that we sometimes must "wonder how not to say the words of love." We do it when we resist an inappropriate love or desire for someone. And, even more puzzling, when we avoid saying "I love you" to someone because we fear the vulnerability we may experience. What if so-and-so does not return my love? What if so-and-so is frightened away by my frank statement of emotion? The line speaks with insight about our mysterious and complicated emotions and needs. Perhaps a third reading hints back to the preceding lines—when one has lost a loved one to death, how can one stop expressing one's intimate connection. The poem does not ask us to return to idealized instinctual ways. It obliquely asks us, I think, to understand and forgive ourselves, while we ironically "shame the monsters."

The second group of poems speak of our moral responsibility to nature, or look for a sense of moral order drawn from phenomena in nature. Mary Oliver's poem "Spring" gives the reader not an observed bear, but an imagined one.

> Somewhere
>   a black bear
>   has just risen from sleep
>   and is staring
>
> down the mountain.
>   All night
>   in the brisk and shallow restlessness
>   of early spring
>
> I think of her,
>   her four black fists
>   flicking the gravel
>   her tongue
>
> like a red fire
>   touching the grass,
>   the cold water.
>   There is only one question:
>
> how to love this world....

By opening with the word *somewhere,* the poet lets the reader know that what follows is speculation in the head, rather than observation in the field. This is an imagined bear and the poem reminds us first of the importance of bear in our imaginations. What would happen to our waking and dreaming consciousness if there were not such a thing as bear. In what ways would our lives be diminished? The poem states that our failure is quite simply a failure of love. Oliver's gift is to see the natural world with a simplicity that seems obvious, but which most of us are too confused or too busy to see without her help. The question is simple: "How to love this world," even if the answers are not readily apparent. This ability to love the world, the poem suggests, is the spring we should hope for—to reimagine ourselves as purely loving.

"Arson" by David Romtvedt begins, again, as a poem of careful and accurate observation of the natural world—the field notebook approach.

> At work we found a rattler.
> The job was to make a rip-rap
> on the desert as if waves
> would someday reach that sea. But it was
> only to stop erosion so men could stand on artificial
> mounds to fire their guns across the air. I don't
> remember thinking the snake would strike. I can't
> remember any fear or idea that I wanted
> to take action. I didn't say a word when another boy
> said, "We have to kill it" and no one disagreed. So we
> did it with stones, at the end striking its head
> like hammering nails to hold targets, hanging
> on to the stone. Then an older man slit its belly
> open, throat to tail, telling stories about other rattlers,
> scrambled eggs and snake brains, being alone
> on the desert. He uncoiled nine unborn snakes, eyes
> still creamlike membrane. They tried to wind themselves
> back round, moving from side to side. It may be they
> were alive or if not, all tropism, some dead creature's
> dance of nerve endings and light. I must not have asked,
> must not have said a thing, just
> looked, learning that rattlesnakes are born

one at a time: the unwinding of the young
on the flat surface of a stone
where they sizzle and pop in the faultless sun.

Romtvedt's field observation clearly takes place in a fallen world. Men are building a platform or stone cobble on an artillery range. They all agree to the necessary killing of a rattlesnake—though there is no apparent threat from this specific creature. It is a generic response to the animal. The author participates as heartily as any of the boys with whom he works and kills. But an insight comes when he sees the pearly baby snakes unwind from the mother snake's slit belly. The little ones wriggle and die on the hot stones. As the author observes this he realizes that "rattlesnakes are born one at a time...," each genetically programmed, neurologically tuned to *want* its life. This insight about the specificity of an individual snake serves as a kind of moral antidote to the generic killing. All that's faultless here is the sun. Until the last line— "where they sizzle and pop in the faultless sun"—we don't know the significance of the title, "Arson." The baby snakes die in the heat of the sun. The sun does the burning, but the speaker rightly claims moral responsibility for the crime.

The next group of poems are works that offer metaphysical speculation about our relationship with nature, poems that willfully work at asking us to reimagine ourselves. First is William Stafford's "Evolution."

The thing is, I'm still
an animal. What is a spirit,
I wonder. But I only wonder:
I'll never know.

Night comes and I'm hungry.
Tempted by anything, or called
by my peculiar appetites,
I turn aside, faithfully.
What comes before me
transforms into my life.

"Truth," I say, and it answers,
"I'm what you need."

I sing, and a song shaped like a bird
flies out of my mouth.

The speaker acknowledges that he is an animal, a moral being, a product and agent of evolution. He has no apparent conflict about his nature. The physical and the spiritual seem balanced and harmonious in this speaker. It is an amazingly unified and peaceful vision of self. He unifies poetry and nature by suggesting that both are means of energy transformation: "What comes before me / transforms into my life." Like Muriel Rukeyser's line "Breathe in experience, breathe out poetry," the passage places the act of poetry making securely in the biological domain. And the poet's song, "shaped like a bird" flying out of his mouth, is an act of creation as tangible and as intangible as the pigeons a magician might pull from his cape.

Pattiann Rogers works the nexus between science and spirituality in a way unique among U.S. poets. She refuses to let her rich scientific knowledge rob her of a sense of celebration and wonder. Her work is informed and inspired by the cosmology of the late twentieth century—and her language draws beautifully from scientific research and discourse. She begins in "Supposition" with the physical.

Suppose the molecular changes taking place
In the mind during the act of praise
Resulted in an emanation rising into space.
Suppose that emanation went forth
In the configuration of its occasion:
For instance, the design of rain pocks
On the lake's surface or the blue depths
Of the canyon with its horizontal cedars stunted.

Suppose praise had physical properties
And actually endured? What if the pattern

Of its disturbances rose beyond the atmosphere,
Becoming a permanent outline implanted in the cosmos—
The sound of the celebratory banjo or horn
Lodging near the third star of Orion's belt;
Or to the east of the Pleiades, an atomic
Disarrangement of the words,
"How particular, the pod-eyed hermit crab
And his prickly orange legs"?

Suppose benevolent praise,
Coming into being by our will,
Had a separate existence, its purple or azure light
Gathering in the upper reaches, affecting
The aura of morning haze over autumn fields,
Or causing a perturbation in the mode of an asteroid.
What if praise and its emanations
Were necessary catalysts to the harmonious
Expansion of the void? Suppose, for the prosperous
Welfare of the universe, there were an element
Of need involved.

We know from neuroscience that the molecules of the brain do physically change to incorporate a new idea or memory. Rogers turns that knowledge around to suppose that our ideas and emotions might physically change the universe. In a preposterous and visionary claim, she speculates that our very purpose might be to infuse the cosmos with praise. We are factories of the tangible stuff called praise. It is a fuel, she postulates, that energizes the very expansion of the universe. Our consciousness has evolved as food for that cosmic hunger. This vision marries contemporary scientific lore with the prior theological notion that God needs us as partners for creation.

Finally, I'd like to close with a discursive and rhapsodic passage from "The Kingdom of Poetry" by Delmore Schwartz. Written in the forties, the poem predates our contemporary doubts about language and our chronic insecurity about the efficacy of our art. He is an ecstatic here and the poem offers a kind of mental equivalent to the gold-lit landscapes of Frederic Church, Thomas Cole, and Asher Duran. Schwartz launches the poem with its title, placing the kingdom of poetry right beside the two other great earthly kingdoms—those of the plants and of the animals. He brings a rapture to the subject that seamlessly unifies poetry and nature, and accounts for that experience of unity in a reinvention of innocence and its inherent attentiveness.

> For it is true that poetry invented the unicorn, the centaur,
>> and the phoenix.
> Hence it is true that poetry is an everlasting Ark,
> An omnibus containing, bearing and begetting all the mind's
>> animals.
> Whence it is that poetry gave and gives tongue to forgiveness
> Therefore a history of poetry would be a history of joy, and
>> a history of the mystery of love
> For poetry provides spontaneously, abundantly and freely
> The petnames and the diminutives which love requires and
>> without which the mystery of love cannot be mastered.
>
> For poetry is like light, and it is light.
> It shines over all, like the blue sky, with the same blue justice.
>
> For poetry is the sunlight of consciousness:
> It is also the soil of the fruits of knowledge
>> In the orchards of being:
>> *It shows us the pleasures of the city.*
>> *It lights up the structures of reality.*
>> *It is a cause of knowledge and laughter:*
>> *It sharpens the whistles of the witty:*
>> *It is like morning and the flutes of*
> *morning, chanting and enchanted.*
>> *It is the birth and rebirth of the first*
> *morning forever.*

EAGLE TRANSFORMING INTO ITSELF

The title of this essay is taken, with gratitude, from the title of a painting by Robert Davidson, a Haida artist from British Columbia.

WHEN I ARRIVE TWO MEN ARE WORKING IN THE CLINIC on an owl. From the tufts on her head, she appears to be a great horned owl. One man sits on a tall lab chair wearing a leather welding jacket and gloves. He holds the bird with her back nestled into his chest, hands securing the legs. The short gleaming feathers that splay out widely at their ends make the bird's coat look almost like silky fur. The eyes are a soft luminous green, roughly the same color value as the blue of semibright sky. The pupil—an intense pool of focus. When the owl turns to look at me through the large plate-glass window, she wastes no energy on distraction, caution, or fear—merely absorbs me in her magnetic gaze. The second man performs the medical procedures, inserting a rectal thermometer, then a feeding tube. During the latter, the handler covers the bird's eyes with a blanket. The owl seems largely undisturbed by the probing and the insertion of plastic instruments. I learn later that she was brought in from town and her injuries include pellets lodged in the wing. The shot has been there a long time and the vet is surprised the owl has lived this long without being able to fly and hunt.

Each raptor (mostly bald eagles, an occasional golden, and a few owls) housed at the rehab center has a clipboard listing its name, the date and place of its rescue, type of injury, nature of the initial damage, and instructions listed under the imperative "Help by Implementing the Following Practices." Most of these birds of prey have become injured or ill because of contact with humans or changes humans have made to their habitat—car or electrical wire collisions, gunshot, feeding on toxic waste in urban dumps, swallowing fishhooks, tangling with fishline, or leg-hold traps. Others, in particular many of the speckled immature eagles, are victims of winter—dehydrated, starving, and exhausted. They are brought here to Sitka from as far away as Fairbanks, though most are rescued within the coastal southeast region of Alaska. The goal is to heal their injuries and release them back into the wild. About forty percent of the residents make it. Some, such as an immature female brought in from Kake with multiple gunshot wounds, are euthanized. Other non-released birds are turned over to captive breeding projects, the fledglings placed outdoors in a handbuilt tower where they can watch wild eagles and learn to hunt, in an attempt to repopulate flagging habitats. Other birds unable to survive on their own remain at the center as educational birds.

One such eagle is Buddy. He was arrested by police in Kake for loitering in a school playground and trying to steal a ball from a child. He arrived at the center in good physical health, but when moved into a mew with other bald eagles, he cowered around the ankles of the handlers. The best guess at his story suggests that he fell from the nest as a fledgling and was rescued by children who brought him home and raised him as a pet. As Buddy outgrew their nurturing, he didn't know how to go wild, having failed to learn the most basic skill of any species—how to bond with creatures of its kind. Having lived for four years at the rehab center, Buddy now cranes his neck and keenly observes the approach of a person coming along the walkway toward his mew. The eagles grouped in other mews may look when a person approaches, but they keep a self-contained dignity. Buddy gawks as if to say, "Hey, what's up? Can I come along?" His injury is human imprinting. It is unlikely that he could survive on his own, particularly as he approaches breeding age. Since this young eagle seems to believe he is a human being (or perhaps that people are eagles), he is likely to direct his courtship behavior at "his own kind." Buddy works in a training program making tethered flights, and his trainers hope that he can be taught to fly free and return. Under his treatment plan is written "Foster human relationship."

I've come this morning to help exercise two bald eagles who are good candidates for release. Shotgun, a local bird picked up drenched and frail on Shotgun Alley, arrived with a drooping wing and a limp probably caused by colliding with a power line. She's been at the center for two months and is not fond of exercising. Three of us, decked out in leather, head for the mew, bringing blankets and a basket of exercise paraphernalia—hood, jesses, wrench, nylon rope fitted with connectors. When we enter the mew, all four eagles jockey tensely from perch to perch, flying into the walls or each other to get out of our way. These four are mature eagles—dark gray bodies, white head and tail feathers, yellow legs and beaks, black talons. An immature bird doesn't look like the same species—for four years or so it bears mottled brown-and-white feathers from head to tail and a black beak.

Jay and Tracy stalk Shotgun with the blankets amid the pandemonium of flapping and thumping eagles. Many have small carpal injuries, bloody scrapes along the wing edge, from hitting the walls. Each eagle is identified with a colored plastic leg band. Shotgun wears the red ankle tag and she, in particular, does not want to be caught. In a lapse of wisdom, she lands on the ground and Tracy approaches, tossing the blanket over the open-beaked head. This quiets the bird, and Tracy folds in the wings, tucking them close to the body, then reaches around for the legs, lifting the captive against her chest. Once Tracy has the bird secured in her arms, Jay slips the leather hood past the beak, snugging it over Shotgun's eyes.

The yellow beak looks immense, as do the black talons. These are the bird's sole implements for hunting, eating, nest building, and self-defense. A simple but impressive arsenal. Three talons meet one that opposes. Open they look almost delicate. But as they close, the single talon slipping like a gear into place among the cogs of the other three, the strength of their grip is sobering. Closed together, they look like a cluster of metal rings. I think of a magician demonstrating, "As you can see, there are no gaps, no means to unlock them once connected." The beak, distinctly yellow against the white feathered head, has a similar precision and strength. The upper beak is hooked and meets the lower with an overbite that must make for the torque needed to catch a flailing salmon, make it airborne, and rip it into meat. (Do they catch prey with the talons or the beak? I realize how little I know about how they survive. I've seen a red-tailed hawk fly with a snake twirling from its claws. All the more impressive—the ability to hunt as if it had eyes in its feet.)

After squishing through a soggy woods path, we get to a football field of muskeg. Rimmed by stretches of tall Sitka spruce and yellow cedar, a snow runnelled peak beyond, the meadow hosts a few scraggly conifers and bleached stumps of adolescent trees. The gray deadwood is draped with misty Spanish moss and tufted with a black variety that looks like fur—as if a bear had rubbed its back against the nubs of rotted, broken limbs. Trees don't take kindly to this waterlogged peatland. Some well-adapted mosses, lichens, and heathers cushion our footsteps. A single white bunchberry flower, similar to the blossom of wild strawberry, leaps out from the drone of browns and olive greens. The wet chill climbs up through the rubber soles of my boots, penetrating my foot bones.

Jay and Tracy work at lacing the leather jesses onto Shotgun's legs, then attaching her by the nylon cord to a wire cable running a hundred yards along the muskeg. The cord is fastened to the wire cable with a repair link and tightened securely with a crescent wrench. Shotgun is not pleased with being confined, and glaring out the crack of daylight at the bottom edge of her hood she lands several gripping bites on Tracy's hand and forearm. Once I freed a gull at the dump, its feet tangled in fishnet. It screamed and screamed until I approached. Then it grew quiet and businesslike, diving its beak into the soft edge of my hand. I was surprised how strong the grip was—painful, though it didn't break the skin. Not, at least, in the time it took me to free its feet. This eagle, I suspect, could break my finger with her lovely yellow beak.

Exercise begins. Time noted. Hood slipped off Shotgun's head. The bird responds to this relative freedom by spanning out her wings and flying, feet dragging the cord, which slips along the cable. She rises only three feet from the ground and after flying for ten feet flops back onto the mossy heath, wings still extended, chest heaving, her exhalations condensing into puffs of rapidly dissipating cloud. Jay approaches, stopping at intervals for the bird to grow used to his nearness. They watch each other with a quiet attentiveness that suggests their mutual curiosity. Each is aware of the damage the other could inflict. Each is aware of another possibility existing between them. Watching their study of each other, I fill up with questions. The eagle clearly is capable of thinking "danger." Is it capable of thinking "help," "care," or "kindness"? Are its mental actions thoughts at all? Does it "think" danger or simply have a bodily reaction to the presence of a predatory species other than its own? Does the eagle have an inner life? Does it dream? Does it "know" that its habitat has shrunk? Does it "want" to fly to the top of a spruce tree, or is it moved by something more akin to magnetic force? Does it "hope" to be free? Does a creature "have" an experience if one lacks the language to describe it?

Overhead a high soaring eagle tilts and descends toward the muskeg, making a number of close passes over Shotgun's exercise trajectory. Once its curiosity is satisfied, it lofts onto the top spire of a tall spruce and stands watching. An eagle on the ground means "there's food here" to other eagles. But I wonder if this eagle, Shotgun, in the company of three human beings means something else to the watcher. Is there an ethos of care, as well as of hunger, within their species? I remember a friend's story about a sparrow who collided with her window and knocked itself out. A second sparrow landed beside the unconscious one—began hopping around, prodding, tending its mate until it woke up.

Shotgun still looks exhausted, slumped in the scrub, breathing slightly less heavily than when she flopped down. It takes a lot more energy for an eagle to get aloft from the ground than for it to soar off the top of a spruce tree. Jay steps closer, lifts the bird upside down by its legs, then gently bracing its breast in his palm, lofts Shotgun into the air. Again, the eagle flaps along the cable run for a few feet and falls gasping to the ground, wings outstretched and trembling. The process goes on for a chilling half hour and Jay, clearly discouraged, says, "She did much better a few days ago. There's something wrong that's not showing up in the blood work or x-rays."

After we carry Shotgun back to the mew, take off the hood, and leave her to walk freely among her mew mates, she shakes her head, glares, and spits in our direction.

The word *mew* derives from the French *muer,* to molt. It originated as a falconry term, referring to a cage for keeping hawks, especially while they were molting. Even the word's literary usages carry the disdain of the captive. Robert Browning: "I've been three weeks shut within my mew." Or Virginia Woolf: "better ... than sitting mewed up in a stuffy bedroom with a prayer book."

A bald eagle in the wild can live for over thirty-five years, though it is not known whether a rehabilitated one will hunt, mate, build a nest—in short, live out its years as a fully authentic bald eagle. One hopeful report is of an eagle recovered in Juneau that had been treated and released thirty-five years ago. One of the handlers tells me that a banded bird was rescued a second time seven years after its initial release. This winter Aretha, a juvenile female blind in one eye who had spent two years at the rehab center, was released on the Skagit River in northwestern Washington. Fitted with a monitoring device, she was tracked by researchers from the Woodland Park Zoo in Seattle using satellite communication. Within a few weeks she had migrated thirty miles downstream from the release site and was feeding on carcasses at a dairy farm. They reported that "while her feeding habits are more opportunistic than predatory, she is adapting fine to her new friends, home, and most important, her freedom." Six months later, she was found electrocuted under a power line. But most released birds, because of researchers' limited funds, are not tracked. Their futures are entrusted to fate and the handlers' faith in the general benevolence of nature.

Bald eagles once lived in every state except Hawaii. Now they are endangered or threatened in all of the lower forty-eight. Biologists estimate there are ten thousand mature bald eagles in southeast Alaska—about the number believed to have lived here before the influx of Russians and Europeans. The immature birds, because of their mottled appearance, are more difficult to count. A national map of fall migration counts made in the late eighties shows a mere sprinkling of sightings on the West and East Coasts, somewhat more promising clusters in Florida, Montana, and the Great Lakes region. On the Flathead River in Glacier Bay National Park annual fall migration counts of bald eagles totaled one hundred eighty-nine in 1965, three hundred in the midseventies, and six hundred in the eighties. Some recovery may have occurred since the banning of DDT in 1973. That pesticide, which becomes more concentrated in body tissues as it moves up the food chain from prey to predator, so weakened the shells of eagle eggs that the embryos could not mature. The population of eagles in Florida plummeted during the fifties and sixties after DDT was sprayed along the coast to control salt marsh mosquitoes. Still, it's difficult to know how to interpret the migration counts. Have the birds retreated to what little old-growth forest (suitable for nest building) they can locate? What about locations where counts were not conducted? What are the trends in the other sites for which only single-year data are available? How many eagles lived in the lower forty-eight before European contact? Only the most mechanistic observer would require these questions to be answered in order to know that the bald eagle is in trouble.

What bald eagles (*Haliaeetus leucocephalus*—"white-headed sea eagle") require to thrive is in direct competition with our species' claims to the land. To breed, eagles must nest. In order to nest, they need a tall tree near water, good clearance for launching and landing, strong open branches for the nest, which may be ten feet wide, and privacy. Eagles generally mate for life and a pair will return year after year to the same nest, adding branches and twigs for structural stability, Spanish moss, weeds, sod, and seaweed for comfort. The trees they favor are ancient hemlock and spruce, often up to four hundred years old, in which they can position the nest high enough for a good survey of the hunting ground. The average eagle pair hatches two eaglets each year, and for three months the parents share the work of hunting prey and carrying it to the nestlings. When food is scarce, only one nestling will survive. Not doggedly mechanistic in their sense of family, sometimes two females mate with one male, together raising four eaglets in one nest.

Their decline has been attributed to loss of habitat, pesticide and toxic waste exposure, and human predation. Protection began in the lower forty-eight under the National Emblem Law of 1940, which forbade killing eagles. Killing bald eagles was encouraged in Alaska with a bounty of two dollars for each pair of eagle feet until 1953. Bounty was paid on more than one hundred thousand bald eagles shot in Alaska between 1915 and 1951. People feared the birds would deplete the salmon fishery, though the birds are more often timid carrion feeders than voracious hunters. Bald eagles are now protected under federal legislation making it illegal to kill or possess any part of an eagle. Penalties range up to ten thousand dollars and two years in jail. It is also illegal to disturb an eagle nesting site. But laws are unlikely to curb the predatory curiosity of a ten-year-old boy out stalking with his brand-new BB gun or the business-as-usual of a logging corporation with its head office in the profit-making clouds.

A hundred years ago, no one would have thought to ask the questions now being answered at the raptor center—how to cure a case of eagle bumblefoot, how to patch an eagle's fractured humerus using a chicken bone and wire, how to flush the dump toxins from an eagle's blood. And, just as important to the eagle's future are the questions being answered about our species—can a human being earn an eagle's trust? what happens to a man who cradles an injured eagle in his arms? what happens to the man when he sets the recovered eagle free?

WHEN I RETURN TO MY SITKA LODGING ON THE SHORE A MILE OUT of town, I see two great blue herons wading in the shallow water and bright green weed of low tide. I am swept into the ballet of their simplest movements—neck extending into forward motion as the long, slow leg begins to rise. The freezing of the water-colored body on the shoreline as fingerlings dart by. Ballet without the ballet master's cruelties—starvation for the long-legged look of grace. How well designed the heron is. A long-legged bird has the equipment to wade in water. But if it possessed, say, a short neck and bill, the bird would be cursed with the ability to get to the feeding ground but the inability to feed. In nature as in home repair having the right tool is everything.

The herons fly up when an eagle lands, two eagles, then glide back fifty feet down shore, the eagles finishing off the herons' meal. Three crows hang around and wait for crumbs. The heron eats by tossing the skinny fish down its equally skinny throat. The eagle takes the same food, clutches it in talons, and bends to rip off bites with its hooked beak. Herons, eagles, crows. How boring the world would be if there were only one bird species and they all hunted the same way.

I remember now my earlier question about how the eagle feeds, whether it captures prey with talons or beak. And luckily I am sitting at a window overlooking Sitka Sound, one of the few places on earth where I can let the question direct my attention to the evidence right outside. These two appear to be snacking at the shoreline by plucking up sand lances or seaweed with their beaks. They display none of the intensity and focus of the hunt, which makes me think they may be plucking only at weeds. For much of the afternoon they stand on the rocks and watch the water, one or the other flapping up to change vantage points or step back from the incoming tide. Out in the deeper channel an eagle descends from a high soar, circling to scan the water, lowering closer to the surface, turning to lead with the talons, arching so the eyes stay on the prey while the feet descend, talons breaking the surface, then the bird rising back up, arching more deeply, leaning to eat midflight the talon-speared catch. On one occasion I saw five or six eagles gathered on a rock for a collective rip-and-feed on what looked through binoculars like a twenty-pound salmon.

Eight bald eagles—now fifteen—now twenty-three dance low along the center of the channel, feeding again and again—dropping down, hovering, lowering, arching, rising, leaning more deeply, rising again to hover, lowering, arching, rising as they follow a school of herring running with the tide. What a party they're having together out there—all dancing to the same music, each taking its turn to dive, all moving forward together, a composition in counterpoint that they might call, had they the words, "The Festival of the Eagles."

Living in the age of experts often makes me fearful that I don't know enough to know what I am seeing. I have been working on eagles for two weeks. More and more I feel that, in the Indian way, the eagles are working on me. What I want to know can be learned with eyes, ears, patience, binoculars, and a library card. Not for me the heroics of the federal biologist flying across the polar icecap with a bush pilot, downing a polar bear with tranquilizer darts, tattooing the paws, and pulling out a molar to find out how old the creature is. Just by sitting in the right place with my eyes opened I can watch a star-mass of eagles whirling hundreds of feet in the air. Each time I try to box off a section of blue sky, to be more scientific and count the gliders, I see that farther up more eagles are soaring, and more beyond them—dark specks barely moving against the high, fair weather clouds. I count twenty— forty—but it's useless to try. The smaller and smaller they get, the more the sky looks like it's eagles all the way up.

Two of the star-mass glide into synchrony hundreds of feet in the air. Wing tips glance, one twirls beneath the other in a half cartwheel, talons up, nearly grasping the talons reaching down from the eagle above it, then flipping upright to soar by its companion's side. This courting goes on for hours—two eagles circling in the abundance of one another's energy, one tumbling underneath, then cartwheeling back into upright flight. I am eager to see for myself the behavior I've read about—the two birds locking talons and falling into a whirling dive, first one then the other tumbling upside down in a kind of trust dance bringing them nearly to the ground. I see only this repeated approach and retreat, an intense mutuality taking place in the sky. A king salmon leaps out of the water, the full length of its body arcing through the air, back-fin taut and translucent in the sun. The eagles don't bother to descend, more interested, for the moment, in entertaining a hunger for each other.

ON THE SATURDAY OF THE RELEASE, A CROWD OF FORTY— maybe sixty—people gather on the beach at Starrigavan Campground. It's the usual human circus of children, dogs, grandparents, videocams, a tour bus painted and finned to look like an orca whale, and a guy handing out newsletters. Three eagle handlers wearing leather jackets and gloves, each holding a hooded speckled bird nestled with its back against the handler, come through the woods to the gravel beach. The birds are Alex, Cupid, and Izzy—the latter named because when he first came to the center, picked up nearly frozen at the town dump, everyone who saw him said, "Is he still alive?"

All three immature birds were victims of winter, rescued during January and February in emaciated and dehydrated condition. The handlers say that the females are more aggressive, feeding first when fish or rats are brought to the mew, having larger beaks and using them to keep unwanted males off the perch. But in this group, Cupid—the only female—is the most laid-back and cooperative. During exercise in the muskeg field, she easily flew the full length of the cable. When picked up and launched she would fly it again and again, straining against the jesses for more lift, the seven-foot wingspan filled like a sail. Izzy, on the other hand, though able to fly, would do so only in one direction and kept pulling off to the left of the cable. He seemed to be irked by the constraints on his legs, unwilling to forget them and fly. I was told that Alex was a feisty bird, vicious when he first was rescued. He ripped clear through the leather sleeve of one handler, and when four rats were set down on the feeding board in a mew with four eagles, Alex scarfed up two. But the day I saw him exercise in the muskeg field revealed a more pensive side of his personality. Alex refused to fly more than a few feet, having just eaten a lunch of trash fish in the mew. His handler, Scott, seemed exceptionally gifted and though he joked, "Let's just set him free today," his patience was beautiful to watch. The bird too seemed to have patience. In between each aborted flight, Alex perched on Scott's wrist, which was raised up to eye level, and the two looked into each other for minutes.

Blue sky and bright sun—an eagle of a day for their release. In preparation the birds have had their talons and beaks resharpened. They had been dulled while in captivity to facilitate handling and prevent further injury in the mews. Alex, who had lost several flight feathers, which will take months to regrow, has had temporary feathers attached through a process called imping, a centuries-old falconry practice. The damaged feather is snipped off leaving an inch or so intact, and a replacement of the same color and aerodynamic design is attached with a bamboo peg held by superglue inside the quill. The process can hasten by several months the release of a bird, reducing the risk of its becoming habituated to human companionship and feeding.

The man with the newsletters asks the crowd to step back and in the usual human fashion some comply while others jockey for the best video vantage. A local Tlingit/Haida woman tells us the eagle is important to her people because it represents the East, which is the direction of wisdom. She beats a drum shaped like a large tambourine and sings an eagle chant passed on to her by an elder. Few of the assembled understand her language or the richness of the native tradition in which animals have the power to communicate spiritual meaning to people. Still, it sobers the crowd to stand in the echo of her singing. The air becomes charged with connection. Finishing, she laughs at herself, "You're supposed to sing it four times, but I'm only doing it once."

One at a time the handlers step forward away from the crowd, each holding an alert, hooded bird. Suddenly, it is my own species I feel sorry for—impoverished by the cruelties we inflict on our own kind and others. And it is my own species that I love for its kindness, watching the little leather hood slip off, the startled eagle confronting the day, launching from the arms of the handler, lifting and banking toward the tall cedars on the edge of the woods, finding a perch, one by one, until three bald eagles disappear into the green.

PERMISSIONS

"Spring" from *New and Selected Poems* ©1993 Mary Oliver. Reprinted with permission of the author.

"Jackrabbit's Ears" reprinted from *Sunflower Facing the Sun* by Greg Pape by permission of the University of Iowa Press. ©1992 Greg Pape.

"The Poem is an animal" from *Unravelling Words and the Weaving of Water* ©1992 Cecilia Vicuña, translated by Eliot Weinberger and Suzanne Jill Levine. Reprinted with the permission of Graywolf Press, Saint Paul, Minnesota.

"Suppositions" from *Expectations of Light* ©1981 Pattiann Rogers. Reprinted with permission of the author.

"Arson" from *Moon* ©1984 David Romtvedt. Reprinted with permission of the author.

"The Kingdom of Poetry" from *Selected Poems (1938–1958): Summer Knowledge* ©1967 Delmore Schwartz. Reprinted with the permission of New Directions, New York, New York.

"Shame the Monsters" from *Apocalyptic Narratives* ©1993 Rodney Jones. Reprinted with permission of the author.

"Evolution" from *Passwords* ©1991 William Stafford. Reprinted with permission of HarperCollins Publishers.

Excerpt from *Make Prayers to the Raven* ©1986 Richard Nelson. Reprinted with permission of University of Chicago Press.

 # ABOUT THE AUTHOR

ALISON HAWTHORNE DEMING IS DIRECTOR OF THE Poetry Center at the University of Arizona in Tucson. She has won many awards for her writing including, most recently, the Walt Whitman Award from the Academy of American Poets, a Pushcart Prize, and a Tucson/Pima Arts Council Literary Fellowship. She has also received NEA and Stegner Fellowships. A book of her poetry, *Science and Other Poems,* was published this spring by Louisiana State University Press.

Editors: Thomas Christensen, Hazel White, and Jenia Walter
Text Designer: Thomas Christensen
Text/Display Type: Adobe Sabon/Monotype Grotesque
Compositor: Philip Bronson
Printing/Binding: Haddon Craftsmen Book Manufacturing